Movement Education

by Robert E. Gensemer

nea
National Education Association
Washington, D.C.

Note

The opinions expressed in this publication should not be construed as representing the policy or position of the National Education Association. Materials published as part of the Developments in Classroom Instruction Series are intended to be discussion documents for teachers who are concerned with specialized interests of the profession.

Acknowledgments

The following materials are adapted and used with permission from the sources indicated: *Basic Movement Education for Children* by Bonnie Cherp Gilliom (adaptations from pp. 54–60 and 150–57), copyright © 1970 by Addison-Wesley Publishing Company; *Teaching Physical Education* by Muska Mosston (adaptations from pp. 107–13 and 202–7), copyright © 1966 by Charles E. Merrill Publishing Company.

Library of Congress Cataloging in Publication Data

Gensemer, Robert E.
    Movement education.

(Developments in classroom instruction)
    Bibliography: p.
    1. Movement education. I. Title. II. Series.
GV452.G46   612'.76   79-1321
ISBN 0-8106-1823-0

Contents

THE BODY HAS A BRAIN 5
We Use It, Then Lose It — The Body Revived — A
Responsive Educational Potential — Meanings and Non-
meanings —

FOR ALL INTENTS AND PURPOSES 10
The Starting Point — Problems Are Opportunities for
Learning — Doing Nothing Is Doing Something — The
Range of Possible Answers Varies — Having a Ball —
Getting Good Service from the Method — A Full
Participation in Learning —

PHYSICAL FREEING 30
The Emancipation of the Inner Person — The Granting of
Freedom — Evaluation Belongs to Students — Information
Comes from Inside —

THE NERVE OF IT ALL 36
A Neural Servant or a Nervous Hindrance — It's the Same
for Everyone — Teaching Better by Saying Less —
Learning to Read Body Signals —

THE INTERNALIZATION OF LEARNING 42
Four Dimensions of Movement — From Inner Space to
Outer Space — The Backside of the Forehand — A Well-
Balanced Person — The Inside of the Infield — A Heavy
Matter — Back to the Backswing — A Long Time Ago in a
Faraway Place — Talking to the Body —

CREATIONS AND CONCLUSIONS 68
Castles in the Air — An Assemblage of Cooperation — A
Carbon Copy — New Wine and New Bottles — Sensing,
Knowing, and Acting — A Carry-Over Consideration —

REFERENCES... 76

RECOMMENDED READING............................. 79

The Author

Robert E. Gensemer is Associate Professor and Director of Graduate Studies, Department of Physical Education and Sport Sciences, University of Denver.

The Consultants

The following educators have reviewed the manuscript and provided helpful comments and suggestions: Richard C. Burnham, Physical Education Specialist, Seattle Public Schools, Seattle, Washington; Dr. John S. Fowler, Coordinator of Undergraduate Physical Education, University of Colorado, Boulder; Dr. David L. Gallahue, Assistant Dean, School of Health, Physical Education and Recreation, Indiana University, Bloomington; Harriet Olson, kindergarten teacher, Lewis Ames Elementary School, Littleton, Colorado; and Dr. Thomas M. Vodola, Director of Research and Evaluation, Township of Ocean School District, Oakhurst, New Jersey.

THE BODY HAS A BRAIN

Think back to an earlier moment in your life — to the time when your parents gave you your first bicycle, all bright and shiny and trim and unscratched and blue (red, green . . .); replete with bulky balloon tires and an uncomplicated one-speed drive; handlebars that flared upward and outward like spindly metal wings; and a big wide, comfortable seat. (Whatever happened to those big, wide, comfortable seats?)

The bike was just your size, your parents had said. But to you it seemed too large. You had tried riding a big two-wheeler before, but you could hardly balance long enough to get the pedals into even one full revolution. Now, however, this one was yours. You *had* to ride it.

And so, in your backyard, you tried. But you had no success. A few days passed. More trials, but still no success. Some friends came over and offered encouragement, but no one can really tell someone else how to ride a bike. You just do it.

And one day you did. On a Sunday afternoon, probably. One of your parents was holding the bike upright and giving you a starting push, just as they had done a dozen times before. But this time, when you were let go, you just sort of did it. Only for three and one-half seconds, but there you were — suspended for the first time in the gyrated ecstasy of being in command of that mechanical contrivance. On the next try you stayed in control for five seconds, then nine, then once around the yard, then several times. Finally you were ready for the street!

Sure, you lost it here and there, and one time in particular you thought you had fractured your left kneecap. But in a week you and your bike had harmonized into freewheeling rhythm — all because of a very natural, seemingly instinctive, human response. You *listened* to your body. However subconscious it may have been, you were receptive to what your own body was telling you. You sensed, experienced, and learned from the information coming to you from your muscles, tendons, and joints. Resultingly, when there was a little loss of balance to the left, you could quickly compensate to the right. When rocks were intentionally placed ahead of you for an obstacle course, you could maneuver skillfully around them. You learned well from that body of yours. In fact, you learned so well that even today your body remembers — you can hop on a bicycle now, and after a few seconds of readjustment you can ride as you did yesterday, even though it may have been decades since you last rode.

5

WE USE IT, THEN LOSE IT

In our youth, we developed effective, relative, and efficient motor capabilities in response to the feeling the body gave us. We learned to climb a tree by climbing a tree, to walk on a fence by walking on a fence, to hit a baseball by hitting a baseball. No one could tell us how to do it quite so well as we could do it ourselves. Self-discovery was the greatest teacher and spontaneity the greatest stimulus. We were our body, and our body was everything we were. We had a true freedom, and an ultimate existence with our own selves.

But given time, and cognitive demands, and cultural roles, and traditionalistic education, we slowly lost most of this contact with the physical self. We first learned to count by using the body; then a calculator took over. We did our first paintings as body expressions; then art became an intellectual thing. When we saw a bug we got down on our hands and knees, examined it, and imitated it; then a microscope did those things for us. Even as adults we have learned to turn off rather than tune in to our bodily sensations. Any drugstore can provide all the pharmacological aids we need to deny our physical experiences.

THE BODY REVIVED

Today, however, there is a growing interest in reanimating the contact we once had with the body. Eastern philosophies have stimulated a great interest in the potential for heightened human experiences that are possible through the body. Zen has worked its way into a wide variety of endeavors, including the teaching process; but it is probably most noticeable in its use, in various forms, as a means of enhancing athletic performance. Professional tennis players now sit at courtside between games and use meditation to help their play. Downhill ski racers mentally and visually rehearse the run before actually executing it. Golfers try to enter a transcendental state while performing.

It is not too surprising to find the athletic world using mind and body togetherness. What is surprising is that it has taken so long for humankind in general to rediscover this harmony. The ancient Greeks knew all about it, as their writings consistently emphasized. For some reason their ideal was lost for several thousand years, however, and now it is here again. After all this time we finally recognize that only one process is going on inside all of us. Mind and body are not separate; mental and physical phenomena are always interrelated, each dependent on the other and each influencing the other. Everyday happenings provide us with the evidence. For example, think of the last time you had a cold. The chances are that you not only felt bad, but you may also have lost your enjoyment of food or reading or other people, and you may have been unusually irritable. As a further example, when you are depressed, your body reflects that state — respiration is more shallow, vitality is lessened, muscles lose some of their coordination, and circulation shows unusual changes (Smith and Smith 1966). And suppose someone suddenly startles you. Where do you sense the surprise? Along the sides of your neck? In your stomach? In your pounding heart? Surprise is an emotion, but you *feel* it physically. Even our common expressions of sensations verify the physical state of our emotions — a lump in the throat, butterflies in the stomach, a pain in the neck.

We also know that people are overt actors of their inner emotional states. We can generally tell, for example, when someone is thinking, or tense, or elated, or tired, or angry. Moreover, we all use body attitudes as a means of emphasizing communications. Patterns of gestures, facial expressions, and other movement activities are symbolic clarifications of what we say, what we think, and what we mean. We become more expressive through movement; thus it could reasonably be concluded that movement is the quantification of our emotions.

In this context, nonverbal communication has recently become a subject of some well-controlled research. The findings of a few isolated studies have stimulated a proliferation of popular books on what is generally called "body language." Other studies have found that physical gestures and body positions can influence the way people respond to each other (Hall 1966) and that body attitudes are often more reliable indicators of the inner self than verbal communication (Fast 1970). Furthermore, physical expression has been successfully used as clinical therapy for maladjusted children and patients in mental hospitals (North 1975), and dance therapy has been used as a positive intervention in the lives of emotionally disturbed persons and autistic children (Rhodes and Tracy 1972).

Finally, there is the intriguing link between mind and body called *biofeedback*. In laboratory settings it has been shown that persons trained in this technique can alter their own brainwave patterns and can consequently influence their own physiological functioning; they can even control muscle activity which we have always believed to be completely involuntary (Brown 1977). The future potential of biofeedback at times seems limited only by our ability to comprehend its power to teach us all how to be totally in control of our mental and physical selves.

A RESPONSIVE EDUCATIONAL POTENTIAL

No one questions anymore the contention that mind and body are not separate. We are, quite clearly, one whole person. There seems to be little doubt that recognizing and accentuating this mind-body togetherness is beneficial to our total functioning. What is most exciting is that the educational process has a means available whereby the awareness of self in students can be heightened through a physical medium. That awareness can then be used to generate an increased capacity for expression, creativity, and self-discipline. These benefits become accessible through a technique of learning called *movement education*. Sometimes referred to as *movement exploration*, occasionally as *educational gymnastics*, and once in a while simply as *movement*, the only accurate description of this learning technique is *movement education*. Its straightforward intent is not only to emphasize the inherent ties between mind and body, but indeed to increase the communication between the two, and subsequently to positively affect one through the other.

MEANINGS AND NONMEANINGS

Movement education. A strange term perhaps. Does it infer some kind of education of movement? Learning how to move? But everybody already *knows* how to do *that*. We can walk to our car, run to get out of the rain, get up to turn on the television, and hit a few softballs at Sunday picnics. We never really needed any formal "education" in how to do those things. What more do we need?

In a more realistic interpretation, movement education does not imply that we all need to be *told* how to perform everyday activities. Instead, it *does* say that we can have educational experiences *through* physical movement and that we can *use* movement as a means for becoming our own best selves. Properly utilized, movement education enhances an awareness of the total self — of the body and its capabilities, and of the psyche, with the body as its expression. As an ultimate achievement, this method develops a consciousness for listening to the sensations the body gives us and also a freedom enabling us to express our inner feelings through the use of the body. We become *receptive* to the information coming to us from the muscle sensors. Thus we can perceptively feel these sensations, and as a final result we can use this information to *direct* the muscles more effectively into a wide variety of performances which can range from free expression to refined motor patterns.

Perhaps this technique could be called *educational movement*, for its basis is that movement is first and most emphatically an *educational* affair rather than merely a productive matter (i.e., the foundational premise is that

8

we can learn *from* movement experiences instead of learning only how to use movement to *produce* skilled motor performance).

This is not to deny that motor skill achievement is desirable. Most certainly, a valid objective of any program which uses movement as its medium is the development of efficient motor skill accomplishment. But such an objective is only a partial ambition; the total concern of movement education is much more encompassing. In fact, it may be one of the very few enterprises which sincerely and legitimately attends to the whole person — to all the mental, emotional, and physical characteristics unique to each individual.

This versatility has already been demonstrated. As exemplification and verification, movement education programs have been shown to be effective in promoting the development of general cognitive abilities (Davis 1977) and increased academic performance (Anthony 1971), in the teaching of reading (Getman 1971) and mathematics (Gilbert 1977), in promoting self-awareness (Snodgrass 1977) and self-discipline (Arnett 1976), in fostering positive self-images (Block 1977), in generating an ability for conceptual thinking (Gilbert 1977), in teaching sports skills (Dochtery 1976), in assisting the general motor development of learning-disabled children (Taylor 1974), in aiding speech development for deaf persons (McDermott 1973), in cultivating motoric and cognitive abilities with mentally handicapped people (Robins 1972), and as a means for facilitating the integration of handicapped children into regular classes (Baker 1973).

How does movement education produce these results?

The essential reason is that the individual is a total person. Mind and body work together. All body messages go to the brain, and all brain affairs are reflected in the body. Everything physical is also a mental matter, and mental activities have body meaning as well.

When you come right down to it, no one is really sure why this is so, i.e., no one is exactly certain why these relationships exist between the mental and the physical. The reason could be neurological, or psychological, or even social; or perhaps all three. It doesn't matter for the moment. What is important is that the relationships exist, whatever the reason.

Periodically, we shall return to this mind-body linkage. For now, we shall put aside theory and take a look at the actual foundation and content of movement education, and consequently see how it can be implemented in the teaching process.

FOR ALL INTENTS
AND PURPOSES

In a broad perspective, movement education designates an individualized approach to motor education with an overall objective of contributing to the effective, efficient, and expressive capacities of each student. It allows for and indeed encourages individuality, spontaneity, creativity, and self-discovery. Its foundational method relies primarily on the concepts of exploration and problem solving.

More precisely, movement education is an open use of the physical medium to promote a multidimensional education. It specifically attempts to provide—

1. Experiences which will enhance conscious perceptual recognition of the sensations that originate from the physical self.
2. An educational environment which will allow freedom and encouragement for the use of the body as a means of expressing states of mind.
3. An educational arrangement which is designed to promote a refinement in the ability to execute purposeful and effective motor responses.

Movement education might be seen as an attempt to "know," to "interpret," and to "direct." It is first an endeavor to know the physical self; then it uses the physical self to interpret mental happenings; and finally it enables one to direct the body into skilled motor performance. *Know. Interpret. Direct.* K.I.D. Kid! That's what most people think movement education is only good for — children. Too many persons are of the opinion that the older the students, the less likely that movement education can be successfully employed with them.

This is not true.

It *was* true when this learning technique was merely a way for teachers to give students an opportunity to run and jump and play and explore and discover and create and all the other ideals of the original concepts. There were no incorrect responses then. A student could do nothing wrong. When someone asked what students were learning from an experience, the answer invariably was that they were learning to run and jump and play and explore and discover and create in some form. The objectives may have been rather nebulous, but they provided numerous opportunities for success and none for failure.

10

Exploration is, in fact, a technique used in movement education to initiate objectives. Discovery is fully anticipated from the way in which the learning environment is arranged. The most celebrated supposed outcome is creativity. Today, however, the reckonings of movement education have gone beyond the mere state of "allowing" certain alleged learnings to take place. Contemporary concerns are more realistically philosophical and include more specifically described educational directions. As we shall discuss later, there is even some neurological support for the very existence of movement education. Moreover, what may be most appealing is the evo-lution of a certain generalized learning technique which is usable in all settings, with all students, regardless of age or previous experiences.

THE STARTING POINT

In the application of its method, movement education begins with the foundation of exploration and problem-solving. This means that a teacher normally presents students with a "problem" which requires an answer to be expressed motorically. Usually, encouragement is given for at least the first motor responses to be of an "exploratory" nature, a sort of trial-and-error which eventually brings students to the self-discovered solutions which are the final objectives. Accordingly, movements are rarely demonstrated by the teacher, since the teacher is not attempting to serve as a model to be imitated, but instead is acting as a catalyst to stimulate student use of motor exploration. Thus students can respond to the situational problem in their own way, within their capacity, and at their own volition. The arrangement is designed to elicit self-initiated motor experimentation which will result in self-appropriated recognition of the most efficient uses of movement.

Most simply, the first of the two basic characteristics of movement education, exploration, might be considered a development of supervised free play. This appears to be the case in the programs which are widely included in the national curricula of England (see especially Briggs 1975). Movement education actually originated in England. (This early development will be discussed later.) The accepted contemporary English version is for the teacher to encourage unstructured free experimentation as a first experience in a learning unit. For example, the teacher might introduce students to gymnastics by arranging some equipment for an initial resolve of allowing everyone to explore the movement possibilities offered by the equipment. There would be no pretense of purpose save that of the exploration itself. Then, in the next stage of the planned progression, the teacher would offer students a series of general challenges such as "Can you

11

find different ways to move around and under the apparatus?" or "Find three different ways to get across the apparatus" or "Discover the parts of your body that give you support as you move on the apparatus."

The English approach to movement education is rather generally oriented toward three concepts: the use of the body (*what* it is that moves), the use of space (*where* it moves), and the quality of movement (*how* it moves). In the implementation of the program, an attempt is made to provide experiences which will give students the self-discovered realizations of what, where, and how their bodies can move. Within these concepts, there is normally no single correct response, but rather a series of possibilities. Encouraged movements are never expected to be stylized but to remain exploratory in nature. In the strictest sense, however, the complete freedom of uninhibited movement which is the introductory phase is replaced by the chain of "suggested explorations" which are directed toward predetermined motor experiences. In some instances, the objective may be for students to ultimately arrive at some rather specific motor responses. Nonetheless, since the "spirit" of exploration is always retained as the primary process in the learning sequence, the products continue to remain self-discovered.

A prevalent feature of the English program of movement education is the liberal inclusion of gymnastic apparatus in the learning scheme. This feature, which provides a very utilitarian setting which blends easily into the avowed objectives, is probably the reason why the program in England has tended to to be referred to as "educational gymnastics."

It is, of course, quite possible to stimulate exploratory movement without gymnastic apparatus, and indeed without any equipment at all. For example, a teacher might say to a group of elementary-age children:

- Let me see you run.

Then:

- Show me if you can run quietly.

And:

- Can you find another way to move on your feet?

This is a very simplified version of the technique of presenting a series of suggestive expressions to students. Usually the stimuli are open-ended, related to each other, and given in progressive order. Thus, such a scheme might be expanded into a whole succession of proposals such as the following:

1. Move around the room in any way that you like.

2. See how many different places you can go to. Have you been to the corners of the room? to the middle? along all the walls? Have you been someplace no one else is?

3. Now, move around the room using a different part of your feet.

4. Can you use just one foot to move?

5. Now, be as heavy as you can as you move.

6. And now, be as light as you can.

7. Make some kind of turning movement as you go around the room.

8. When I clap my hands, freeze yourself into any position you like.

9. Now, move in any way that you wish again; and as you move, try to stay as far away from everyone else as you can.

10. Move as fast as you can, still staying away from everyone else.

11. Now, find a space on the floor, away from everyone else, and let your weight sink down to the floor.

12. Find different ways to support your weight on the floor.

13. Have your body supported by four parts; now, three; now, two; now, a different two.

14. And now, move around the room again, slowly, and support your body on different parts as you move.

15. Move in as low a position as you can.

16. Can you now move in a high position?

17. Can you make your body go from a high position to a low position and then to a high position again?

18. See if you can get your feet high off the floor and then land on them softly.

19. And now, in your own space, keep your feet still and stretch your arms out as far as you can without touching anyone else.

20. Move your hands to all parts of your own space.

21. Try to get your hands as far away from the rest of you as you can.

22. How big a space can you use by stretching out your whole body?

23. Now, keep your hands on the floor and find all the places you can move your feet into.

24. Keep your hands on the floor, lift your feet into the air, and bring them down at a different place.

25. What different shapes can you make with your whole body?

As the sequence continues, it begins more and more to take on (and sometimes to become indistinguishable from) the second foundational characteristic of movement education — problem solving. In a very real sense, a question such as "Can you change speeds as you move around the room?" or some similar solicitation is actually the presentation of a "problem" which can only be answered motorically. There can literally be no "wrong" answer in such an open-ended proposal; neither is there a single "correct" response. However, as we shall see in later examples, the problem-solving technique can be used to elicit rather specific motor behaviors, particularly when it is utilized with older students.

PROBLEMS ARE OPPORTUNITIES FOR LEARNING

A problem, in a classical sense, is a question or situation proposed for consideration or solution. Generally, when a problem-solving endeavor is employed in education, it carries with it the trait of a possible solution. That is, any problem which is given students should have a discoverable answer, no matter how liberal the allowances may be. This feature distinguishes problem solving from pure exploration, and actually gives the hint of a right-wrong dichotomy. However, "rightness" or "wrongness" is in reality an informational guide for teachers and students to use toward the development of effective motor behaviors. For instance, the teacher may begin a tennis lesson with inexperienced players by saying, "Pick up the racket in any way that you like and swing it around in any direction you wish." This is a totally nonstructured suggestion without the intent of a prescribed product. The teacher did not actually present a "problem," and the request is purely one of becoming acquainted with the feel of the racket in the hand. Then, the teacher may begin to narrow the range of motor operations and direct students toward more specific ends. The next statements might therefore be similar to the following: "How do you think you would need to swing the racket to hit a ball in that direction?" or "Do you suppose there is a best way to hold the racket to hit a ball on this side of your body?" or "What would happen to a ball if you hit it when your racket was going in this direction?" Further examples could be seen in a volleyball class when an initial statement such as "See if you can keep the ball in the air" becomes "What is the best way to get the ball over the net without catching and throwing it?" Or, in basketball, the invitation "Let me see you bounce the ball" becomes "What do you need to do to keep other players from getting the ball while you are bouncing it?" In using a balance beam the proposal "Try finding different body positions as you balance" becomes "If you move one body part to the side of the beam, what do you need to do to keep your balance?" It is all a matter of increasing the muscle awareness and promoting more effective quality of movement through mere verbal suggestion. The teacher always stimulates, never tells, and the *process* remains one of exploration. In essence, the students are on their own, given freedom from time imperatives and teacher dictates. They therefore become responsible for their own motoric organization.

Accordingly, at this point in our discussion, we can draw a few conclusions about the foundational methodology of movement education as applied to any setting and with any age group.

THE INITIAL EXPERIENCES ARE PROVIDED AS AN ALLOWANCE AND ENCOURAGEMENT FOR TOTALLY UNSTRUCTURED EXPLORATION.

And then in the progression of the method:

THE TEACHER PRESENTS "PROBLEMS" WHICH REQUIRE MOTORIC ANSWERS.

Always, however:

THE PROCESS OF EXPLORATION REMAINS THE MEDIUM OF LEARNING.

At first there is only the doing; then there is the presentation of designed challenges to which students respond with motoric experimentation. This sequence can be used in virtually any activity; and it can be employed with all skill levels, novice to advanced.

The following example demonstrates how this straightforward technique might be applied by a teacher with students who are having a first experience with parallel bars. (In the absence of parallel bars, it could be adapted to a vaulting box, or a side horse, or a simple bench.) It could begin with the direct query:

1. How do you get on the parallel bars?

This seems like a simple, innocent enough question. At this point it is merely an open-ended request for exploration. It is a logical starting consideration, for to do anything on parallel bars means that a student must first get *on* them. However, this impassive little inquiry may contain the possibility of too many solutions. Climbing one of the supports *does* get a student on to the parallel bars but is not very economical and does not give the student an opportunity to learn something about the relationship between body, bars, space, and movement. Therefore, it may be necessary for the teacher to be suggestive about the available solutions such as

2. Can you discover a way of getting on the bars by jumping?

3. Is there a way for you to jump and finish with your weight being supported by your hands?

4. Can you perform a mount which will finish with your weight entirely on one bar?

5. Try starting from a standing position, in the middle of the bars, and finish with most of your weight resting on one of the bars.

6. Is there any rotary motion which will help you get on the bars?

7. Can you begin your mount from a position other than standing?

8. Find a way of getting on the bars in which you end with most of your body higher than the bars.

9. Can you begin a mount by standing with your back to the bars?

10. Try to make changes in the speed and rhythm of your mounts.

The intent is never to restrict students but to illustrate that there are different, dynamic, and numerous acceptable methods of achieving the same end. Then, when students have experimented with ways to get on the parallel bars, the teacher might suggest:

11. Can you find a position in which your body is supported vertically?

12. How many different parts of your body can be used to support yourself on the bars?

13. Can you support yourself with your hands and then do some kind of swinging motion?

14. Find a way of supporting yourself in which all the joints of your body are bent.

15. Which parts of your body would be unsafe to use as a support?

16. Can you do a maneuver in which you finish in an upside-down posture?

17. Can you do a trick in which your body starts on top of the bars, then goes below the bars, and finishes on top of the bars again?

18. Start on one bar and do a maneuver in which you finish with your weight on the other bar.

19. Are there circular motions you can use to move along the bars?

20. Can you develop a sequence of movements which includes a change of direction?

The suggestions could continue almost indefinitely and could center on emphasizing the various body parts which can be used for support, or the various body positions from which one can move (or end), or the relationship of the body to the bars, or the kinds of movement that can be used. A whole series of suggestions can then be introduced relative to the manner in which one could get *off* the bars.

Gymnastic equipment is a great medium for students to learn about the movement capabilities of their bodies. However, it also seems particularly vulnerable to certain "standard" performance criteria. Over the years a number of "accepted" maneuvers have appeared which probably emanate from competitive settings and which almost invariably seem to be found in the teaching of gymnastics in nearly every learning situation. These prototypes cannot be used by a movement education teacher as formal objectives for experiences in gymnastics. Perhaps in certain circumstances they can be used as models to assist in skill refinement, but they should never become earmarked as final indicators of achievement for all students.

DOING NOTHING IS DOING SOMETHING

An important element to recognize at this point is that movement education requires patience. The teacher who establishes a problem-solving situation for students must then have the forbearance to await the anticipated responses. Problem solving is first of all a process of cognitive organization. Before students can act, they must first think. Since thinking is a very individual event, some students may be quite slow to react, perhaps studying the situation longer than others and needing additional time for organizing their perceptions. This might place some psychological stress on a teacher who believes that *something* ought to be happening. In fact, something *is* happening, for in this interval students are engaging in the free-lance mental arrangements which are the necessary first component to discovering solutions. This information processing (studying the "facts" of a problem) *must* occur before responses can be attempted. It appears to be an essential start to *every* problem-solving situation (Newell and Simon 1972), and it is also apparent that this preliminary organizing of thoughts operates on a different time continuum for all persons (Scandura 1977). Thus the teacher must be willing to do nothing in the beginning, allowing students to do a constructive search in their own minds.

It is also evident that a necessary second step in problem solving is trying out a variety of possible solutions (Maltzman 1960). This is a kind of operational trial and error during which potential answers are attempted. Consequently, a teacher must not only allow each student the time needed to collect his/her thoughts, but must also permit the first responses to be completely volitional. Of course, this process might take an unreasonable amount of time; when this happens the teacher must enter the picture by assisting students in selecting feasible operations. The aid given by the teacher at this time, however, must be confined to open-ended suggestion and guidance, never the providing of end answers; for research indicates that the only significant learning in problem-solving experiences comes from personal self-operation in (and on) the situation (Rickards 1974).

THE RANGE OF POSSIBLE ANSWERS VARIES

When the objective of movement education is the development of particular motor skills (rather than pure exploration), the extent of potential responses becomes narrowed by the nature of the skill being taught. With some skills there may be only a very small range of effective responses, while with others there may be no allowance at all for variation at certain stages of the performance. For example, hitting a golf ball straight demands that at the moment of contact, the center of mass of the clubhead must be directly behind the center of mass of the ball, with the clubhead perpendicular to the intended line of flight of the ball while travelling directly on that line. It's a matter of physics. No matter how restricting it may be, one simply cannot violate the physical laws which govern the effect of a moving clubhead on a stationary golf ball. Physics includes a knowledge of consequences, and we all know what happens when we swing a golf club in erratic fashion.

Nonetheless, the principles of movement education can still be used for the learning of a skill as exacting as golf. The whole matter is resolved by the fact that it is not necessarily the *product* which is unique to movement education, but the *method* which is used for teaching. Exploration and problem solving can apply to the learning of *any* skill. To illustrate, two examples follow — one in which problem-solving experiences are used in a skill which allows for variation in performances (soccer) and one in which the performance demands are quite rigid (a topspin tennis serve).

HAVING A BALL

It *does* seem that the principles of movement education are particularly well suited to activities in which there is a constantly changing environment. In such situations the versatility of the performer is valuable. A basketball game, a field hockey match, a football game, a lacrosse game, and similar sports are in ever-constant flow, never exactly duplicating the previous moment. Participants are required to constantly adapt.

Responding appropriately to changing environmental demands is a human ability that apparently can be facilitated and appears to be best learned through the presentation of variable and situational problem-solving circumstances (Gilbert 1978). Ball games are excellent examples. The problem-solving demands are dynamic — always changing. Player responses must be variable, adaptable, and available.

In the following illustration, exploratory problem solving is used to promote the learning of soccer skills. The example is adapted from Mosston (1966, pp. 207–13), whose book remains one of the best guides available to help the teacher develop and use a problem-solving methodology.

The game of soccer itself, like most other ball games, is a series of relationships — between players, the ball, opponents, and the field. Thus the game can be considered from the standpoint of possibilities presented by the relationships. A soccer player may discover that a given relationship (i.e., the position of the ball and the opposing players at a certain moment) may offer several possibilities and that within these possibilities there are preferences — solutions to the situation which are more economical or profitable than others. Additionally, there may be an underlying concept which will influence matters. For example, if a team is playing a particular offensive or defensive alignment, it may somewhat limit the possibilities available to individual players in favor of preserving the overall concept.

Notwithstanding these considerations, one of the inherent values of the game of soccer is that it encourages participants to play with a definite degree of flair, no matter what the level of play. The variations within the game are continual, and the moments are always changing. Virtually nothing is static; therefore considerable individuality and versatility are allowed the players. And yet, although the relationships are forever new, they are always familiar enough to an experienced player so that the possibilities at any moment are never unrecognized. Correspondingly, for a novice player, soccer can offer a sequence of problem-solving situations which require the same relevant responses demanded of the accomplished performer.

The teacher might begin a lesson in soccer by first presenting the most fundamental of relationships, that of player and ball. If the learners are inexperienced, the situations could be offered in a sequence somewhat like the following:

1. Show me how you can get the ball from here to there. (With this invitation some students may pick up the ball and carry it, others may throw it, etc.)

19

2. Is there a way that you can get the ball from here to there by using just your lower body? (At which most of the students will probably give the ball a kick.)

3. Can you now get the ball from here to there, using only your feet and moving along with the ball as you do it?

4. Try this time to keep the ball rolling along the ground as you move it.

5. Can you move the ball along the ground, using only your feet and keeping it very close to you?

6. Is there another part of your body besides your hands that you could use to move the ball?

7. Now, try to move the ball from here to there, using any part of your body you wish except your hands.

8. Which body parts seem easier to use? Which give you more control of the ball? Why?

9. Which body parts could be used to make the ball go a great distance?

10. And now, suppose you were playing a game where other players were trying to take the ball away from you. Show me how you would move the ball to keep the other players from getting it.

At this point if there is available space, and if the teacher has the fortitude to try it, have students move the ball anywhere they want, in any fashion they wish, simply trying to encourage different techniques as they experiment with the ball. Then, after the player-ball relationships have been explored, attention might be given to the more specific effects of the foot on the ball.

1. What parts of your foot can you use to move the ball from one place to another?

2. Does it seem that certain parts of your foot will give you more control of the ball than others? Which ones? Why?

3. How can you touch the ball, now, to make it go on a straight line while still keeping it close to you?

4. What must you do to the ball to move it to your right, still keeping it under control?

5. Can you do the same thing to move the ball to your left?

6. Is there more than one way to make the ball change directions while keeping it near you all the time? still another way?

7. Find out which part of your foot seems to be best for making an accurate short kick.

8. Now, use the same part of your foot and try to kick the ball very hard. Does it seem that another part of your foot would be better for this type of kick?

9. What happens to the ball if you kick it with your toe below its center?

10. Is there another way to get the ball to fly into the air?

11. Find out what happens if you take a few running steps before you kick the ball.

12. Now, try the same thing, this time using your weaker leg. Is there a difference in what happens to the ball?

13. Is there a type of kick you can do well with your weaker leg?

14. Push the ball away from you and try to make it stop on that spot over there. Now, use a different part of your foot to do the same thing. Does one technique work better than the other?

15. Keep your ankle very stiff when you kick the ball. Then keep it very relaxed. Which seems to work better?

So far the situations have involved the *propulsion* of a soccer ball. The game also requires that players be able to *receive* a moving ball. Therefore, the teacher might next design a series of problems concentrating on that aspect.

1. Does anything change, now, if the ball is rolling toward you on the ground?

2. Pass the ball to each other on the ground, and see what you need to do to stop the ball.

3. Use different parts of your foot each time the ball comes to you.

4. Have you discovered which part of your foot you can best use to stop a moving ball? Can you make the ball stop right in front of you using this part of your foot?

5. What must you do to stop a ball that is coming to you from your right side? from your left? Try to make each ball stop very close to you as you experiment.

6. Can you stop and control a ball that is coming from behind you?

7. Can you bring a ball moving away from you under control?

8. Discover what you can do to stop a moving ball, and then quickly get it ready to move away from you again.

9. See if you can move a ball that comes to you on the ground quickly away from you again without actually stopping it.

10. What changes do you need to make, now, to stop a ball coming to you slightly off the ground? high off the ground?

11. Are there parts of your body other than your feet which can be used to stop a ball that is bouncing toward you?

12. Can you stop a bouncing ball, put it under your control, and then get it quickly away from you again? How many different parts of the body could be involved?

13. If a ball is coming to you high over your head, is there a way that you could get it quickly away from you again without letting the ball hit the ground before you do so?

14. If the ball is rolling toward you on the ground, how can you stop it, control it, and then move it along the ground yourself, staying with it all the time?

15. If the ball is rolling toward you on the ground, what must you do to quickly kick it away from you, making it go into the air as you do so?

Next, the situations could focus on the element of *motion*, that is, having both the learner and the ball in motion simultaneously.

1. Can you move the ball along the ground, then stop it, and turn around and move the ball back to where you came from?

2. See if you can move the ball fast, then slow, then fast again. Change speeds as you feel like it.

3. Try to touch the ball with your right foot, then your left, then your right, and so on, as you move the ball.

4. Use only your weaker foot to move the ball on the ground.

5. Now, move the ball around the field in any way that you like, trying to stay as far away from all the other players (who are also in motion) as you can.

Then the relationship of a *teammate* could be introduced.

1. If you wanted your partner to be able to control the ball, should you pass it along the ground or in the air? Why?

2. Can you and your partner make the ball go back and forth between you as quickly as possible while still keeping it under control?

3. Can you and your partner move the ball between you, using body parts other than just your feet?

4. Now, you and your partner try to keep the ball in the air as much as possible, allowing it to bounce only once between each touch of the ball.

5. If the two of you are far apart, how should the ball be passed to each of you? What if you are very close?

Now, motion can be used again as both players (or more) and the ball are all moving.

1. As you move the ball along the ground, can you pass it to another player who is also in motion?

2. How do you need to pass the ball to make sure the other player does not need to stop to receive it?

3. Now, you and your partner move the ball up and down the field in any way that you like, sometimes close to each other and sometimes far apart. Which way would be better if you were trying to keep the ball away from other players?

4. Of course, in a game there will be other players trying to take the ball away from you. So let's now have a third player try to get the ball from you while you and your partner move the ball around the field. Do you need to do things differently? What are some of the things that seem to work best?

5. And now, we'll have a second player also trying to take the ball away from the two of you. Are there things that you could do before that you can't do now? What can you do when you do not have the ball to help your partner who has the ball?

Finally, this learning scheme can evolve into the more complex situations of the actual game. In this respect, learners will not only need to recognize relationships and possibilities, but also preferences and concepts. The movement of a soccer team in a competitive game is not a haphazard affair; it proceeds in a fashion which maintains a number of concepts.

1. Suppose you have the ball, near your opponent's penalty area, and two defenders are marking (guarding) you. What does this tell you immediately?

2. You are in control of the ball, right in front of your own penalty area, but several opposing players are very near you. What are some of your choices?

3. Your team is ahead by two goals in the second half of a game. What might all of you do that would be different from what you would do if you were behind in the game?

4. What is a general thing to do to an opposing player who has the ball in your half of the field near the sideline?

5. Suppose you are marking an opposing midfielder who has the ball. Do you do anything differently as the player comes closer to your own goal? Suppose the player is faster than you are? slower? taller?

This inquiry method could, of course, be used to teach any other segment of the game (heading, goalkeeping, etc.). It requires that the teacher provide a rather artful organization of the environment and probably also requires a graphic use of language. Certainly, a knowledge of the game of soccer itself is imperative so that the learning experiences may be realistically arranged.

What is actually being done in these situations is to narrow and convert real game occurrences into problems for learners to solve. Soccer is a very fluid game, however, and it may seem to lend itself more readily to problem-solving learning experiences than other activities which are more structured. For example, can the same exploratory method be used to facilitate the learning of skills in which movement patterns are more rigidly prescribed, as in golf, diving, bowling, archery?

Of course it can.

GETTING GOOD SERVICE FROM THE METHOD

Serving a tennis ball effectively is a skill which is predicated on certain laws of physics. Getting the ball to go to an intended place is no accident. It requires that the racket be brought into the ball in a very ordered fashion — the face must be at a certain angle, the ball must travel a determined path — because of mass and momentum, action and reaction, angles of rebound. It is an interaction of two moving objects, racket and ball, based on *absolutes*; that is, the laws of physics involved will not tolerate variances in execution. Then, if we add the further dynamics necessary to impart spin to the ball, we have for consideration a skill which demands very narrow channels of movement requirements for successful execution. Indeed, learning a topspin serve in tennis seems to be a guarantee of instant frustration, for it may possibly be one of the more difficult of all sports skills.

Assume now that we were to eavesdrop on a teacher who is using a problem-solving methodology to teach the topspin serve to a group of students who are experienced tennis players but who have not yet tried such a serve. The hypothetical conversation might go something like the following:

TEACHER: Today I would like all of you to try a new kind of serve. It's different from what you have been doing, because we are going to try to put a great deal of spin on the ball. Can anyone imagine why we would want to do that?

CONNIE: I think it's to make the ball take a weird bounce, and it's harder for the other player to hit it back.

TEACHER: Well, that's actually one of the reasons. But first, let's consider what happens to the ball in the air before it bounces. We could compare it to a baseball curveball. Does anyone know what happens to a baseball when a pitcher throws a curve?

BOB: The ball doesn't go straight. It curves. I mean, it goes like this. (*He gestures in an arc with his arm.*)

TEACHER: That's exactly right. The ball takes a curving path. And if we could get a tennis ball to do that when we serve it, would that be an advantage?

MICHELE: I think so, because it would kind of move away from the receiver. It would go to the side of the court, and the receiver would have to reach way out to the side to hit the ball.

TEACHER: That's true, at times. It depends on how the ball is hit. But suppose we could get the ball to spin like this — that's what is called topspin, or overspin. What would that make the ball do in its flight?

25

DONNICA: It seems like it would come down.

TEACHER: Exactly. And why would that be of benefit?

HARRY: Because it would mean that the ball is coming down toward the court. And it would have a better chance of going in the serving area.

TEACHER: Yes, you're right. Just as a baseball curves when it is thrown with spin, a tennis ball which is hit with spin will travel in an arc. And if the ball is hit so that it has topspin, the path of the ball will be downward. That's a great advantage when serving, because it gives the ball a much better probability of going in the service court. Now, here's the critical question — how do you get a ball to spin like that?

CONNIE: You'd need to slice it. I mean you'd need to hit it like this. (*She makes a chopping motion on a ball.*)

TEACHER: Your reasoning is right. To make the ball spin you need to hit it with a glancing blow. But what will happen to the ball if you strike it along the side, as you are suggesting?

DONALD: It would curve to the side. Not really downward.

TEACHER: That's right. And now, what do you need to do to the ball to make it curve downward? How must it be hit to give it topspin?

JERRY: You'd have to hit the top of it.

TEACHER: That does seem logical, doesn't it? But if we actually hit the top of the ball, it would make it go straight down in front of us. And we want to put the ball into that court over there.

CONNIE: Oh, I see what you mean now. The ball must be hit on the opposite side from where you want it to go. So you'd need to hit the back of the ball. Or maybe at the back and a little along the side, but mostly the back.

TEACHER: You're right. And then to give the ball topspin, in what direction must the racket be moving at the time of contact with the ball?

SUE: I'd say upward.

26

TEACHER: Yes, exactly. To give the ball topspin it must be hit at its back surface, with the racket moving in an upward direction at the time of contact. That's what will make the ball rotate as we want it to. It may seem like that's the wrong thing to do, since the racket is moving up, yet we want the ball to go mostly forward. I think, now that what might be best at this point is for all of you to try it. I'd like you to toy around with this idea, and see if you can make the ball leave your racket with topspin. You'll probably need to try several ways of hitting it, and the flight of the ball can give you cues as to what changes you may need to make. Let's all find a space behind the baseline and hit about two dozen serves or so, and then we'll reassemble to find out what we have learned so far.

(Students disperse around the courts and begin their experimentation with the serve. While they are hitting, the teacher circulates among them, never telling them how to hit the ball but sometimes making suggestions about what they might try. After fifteen minutes, the teacher calls them together again.)

TEACHER: What are some of the things you have discovered during this trial period?

DAVID: Mostly that I can't do it.

JANET: I think every ball I hit went up in the air.

ALBERT: Me, too. I hit several over the fence.

DONNICA: I just don't understand how we can make the ball go in that direction *(pointing to the service court)* when we are swinging the racket upward like this. Everything I hit went in the air, too.

TEACHER: OK. That actually tells us something. It shows that we need to make some sort of adjustment to hit the ball in the direction we want it to go. Any suggestions?

BOB: Well, I found out that if I tilt my racket a little, it will keep the ball from flying too high in the air.

MICHELE: I did, too. But I didn't know if I should hold the racket differently or just bend my wrist more or what.

TEACHER: You have figured out part of it. The racket must be tilted forward somewhat to compensate for the fact that it is moving upward when it strikes the ball. This tilt will keep the ball from being hit in the air. And now let's see, how can we best make the change?

27

HARRY: Couldn't you just change the way you are holding the racket?

TEACHER: Right. Now, let me help you all a little. If you will each hold your racket in a grip that is halfway between your own forehand and your own backhand, this will tilt the racket at just about the right angle. Hold the racket up in the air, now, and see the difference. This is one of the most important changes you need to make when hitting a topspin serve. Take a few serving swings and notice the feel it gives your arm.

JERRY: I've got a question that maybe relates to this. Someone once told me that you must toss the ball back further to hit a topspin serve. Is that really true?

TEACHER: Yes, it is. And it does relate to this. Do you know why you must toss the ball further back?

JERRY: No, not exactly.

DAVID: That doesn't make much sense to me. I think if you tossed the ball back further, you'd be hitting it up in the air again.

MICHELE: Maybe not, I was trying that awhile ago, too. And it seemed that if I tossed the ball back further, it made me swing more upward.

DONNICA: Hey, that's right! I was doing my normal toss and I didn't feel as if I could swing up on the ball as we were supposed to because the ball was so far out and away from me.

TEACHER: Great! You are all making excellent observations! Now let's see — what we are all saying here is that there is a relationship between where you toss the ball and the potential for a successful serve. So, if we really do toss the ball back further than we are accustomed to doing, what do you suppose . . . .

Of course this chain of problematical circumstances could be continued to include the total mechanics of the topspin serve. It could also be used to teach a forehand drive. Or a crosscourt backhand. Or a drop volley. Or game strategy. Or any other aspect of tennis play. It is a matter of the teacher's ability to fill the air with stimuli which will result in the experimental solving of motoric problems. And *that*, clearly, is an art.

A FULL PARTICIPATION IN LEARNING

An older (yet still time-honored) practice of education is to give students problems and then expect that they will pull out some prepackaged rule or concept previously committed to memory. This practice consists of the teacher asking and the students answering. This is not necessarily an ineffective arrangement. The process of movement education, however, quite simply alters the way in which the original information becomes established in the beginning. In the traditional approach to education, students are given solutions before they are presented with the problems. That is, first, the facts are generally offered; and, second, the application of those facts is revealed — a standard two-stage process. Movement education reverses these events. In exploratory learning, students first become involved in the problems; then, the solutions become a product of that involvement. Instead of having students solve a problem by applying already known facts (which may have been supplied by a teacher), movement education imposes the problem on students without first supplying the answer. What this procedure does, in essence, is to place a greater responsibility for learning on students, for it generates a greater involvement in the process itself. Learning cannot take place in this arrangement unless students *are* involved. The teacher does not act as an outside source of information, but instead becomes a catalyst for each student to be his/her own teacher and learner simultaneously. This procedure affords a far greater and more holistic involvement in the learning process — and there isn't much question among learning theorists that when students are *involved* in learning they are more likely to acquire and maintain knowledge (see especially Gagné 1970). Moreover, in the implicit sense of the word, "involved" means that students are *in* the learning process, becoming part of it. There is a total interaction. What is most intriguing is that the research indicates that when this total interaction includes the physical medium, the learning which occurs is more meaningful and more readily acquired (see especially Travers 1973). This situation is no different from doing some shopping. We have a hard time just *looking*. Instead, we handle the material the slacks are made of, or pick up a frying pan, or squeeze the grapefruit, or maybe even kick a tire. We do so because we want as much information about a product as we can get, and we find that our bodies can provide us with this data.

Movement education affords meaningful learning in that it allows students to be both cognitively and motorically involved. Students become directly associated with the mental-motor hookups which are the foundation of conceptual understanding. They are not asked to exist outside themselves, as is true in the more traditional method whereby the teacher may provide them with responses. Rather, there is an internalization of the whole process and, in the truest sense, an *active* involvement, both covertly and overtly. The resulting learnings are thus more meaningful for students.

PHYSICAL FREEING

There is a precaution to be noted here. If the self-appropriated learning technique which movement education promotes is truly to work, a rather significant sacrifice is required of the teacher. The sacrifice is more than one of time or energy or values. Rather, it is one of domination. Movement education is an *allowance*. In this context a teacher must have a *willingness* to give students permission for the unhindered exploration of their own resources. In a very real sense this means that the teacher must be inclined to give up some "control" of students and pass the responsibility for that control to the students themselves.

This sacrifice may be difficult for some teachers to make. It involves a sort of "letting go" of some authority which might conceivably be viewed as being inconsistent with the presumed protocol of education. Moreover, such a sacrifice seems to include a built-in loss of some of the "power" that is assumed to come with the role of teacher. The effect could be that the relinquishing of authority represents not only a threat to one's jurisdiction, but also an open invitation to chaos.

Some research evidence supports this contention. In a comprehensive and highly revealing investigation of the teaching process, Dunkin and Biddle (1974) have shown that there is a tendency for most teachers to feel insecure about situations which appear to be structureless. There is apparently a rather general feeling among teachers that "something ought to be happening" virtually all the time in any educational setting, and the open allowances which are the requisites for movement education do not seem, at least on the surface, to provide the ordinances for such events. Consequently, the interplay of these perceptions may often lead teachers toward a more directed regulation of classes and a correlated hesitation with respect to anything as open-ended as movement education.

Nonetheless, movement education *requires* that the atmosphere be one of liberty — a feeling of independence for students. A real *sense* of being free must be accorded students before the method can be tried. In effect, then:

THE SUCCESS OF A PROGRAM OF MOVEMENT EDUCATION DEPENDS, FIRST OF ALL, ON THE ESTABLISHMENT OF AN EDUCATIONAL ATMOSPHERE OF FREEDOM.

This does not mean the mere giving of uncommitted time to students. Rather, it is a psychological *feeling* of being without any externally imposed restrictions.

THE EMANCIPATION OF THE INNER PERSON

All of us endeavor to be free from constraining situations and uncomfortable events. We want, for example, to be free from cold or noise or crime or crowding. Even a cough or sneeze or eating is a reduction of aversive stimuli.

A more important kind of freedom, however, is that which can exist in our minds as a psychological attitude. This freedom is of a far greater dimension and can only be an actuality when an environment has been intentionally arranged to permit the full expression of individuality. Such a setting would allow for the openness, the spontaneity, and the creativity which are manifestations of the inner person.

The most important requirement of such an atmosphere is that the environment be nonjudgmental. Essentially, teachers must lay aside their opinions and give students a liberty which results in their *feeling* and *knowing* that they are free to think and to respond in their own way and with their own intuitions. This atmosphere can only be established by removing threats from the environment, the most imposing of which would be the fear of being wrong.

Actually, more is required. There should also be an *encouragement* of individuality. All students have states of mind, feelings, traits of character, intentions, purposes, and other personality factors which make each one unique. In an atmosphere of honest freedom, students are actually expected to demonstrate these qualities. Movement education, therefore, not only encourages originality but in fact *expects* it. In this respect, teachers become catalysts for the fostering of original thought and the generation of spontaneous experimentation. Teachers cannot *tell* students how to respond; they must instead provide *stimuli* for self-generated learning.

In an atmosphere of freedom, the individual's spirit becomes liberated. Each student becomes the mediator of cause and effect, being the *center* from which individual behavior emanates. Each student initiates, creates, and judges, and in so doing begins with self and ends with self.

As related specifically to motor behavior, freedom permits students to manifest their own movement patterns, with the obligation of responsibility only to themselves instead of to a teacher who might be telling and showing specified (and expected) motor performances. In contrast, a teacher who demonstrates storybook skill executions for students to observe, and then anticipates that students will mimic those executions, operates on the erroneous belief that all students are anatomically and neurologically identical and therefore would learn motor behaviors in exactly the same manner. But all people are cast from different molds. We are all individuals — not only anatomically, not only emotionally, not only attitudinally, but also *neurologically* (see especially Leukel 1978). Sensory phenomena vary within all of us. Most importantly, our motor organization is ours alone, no one else's. The way in which we perceive sensory stimuli, cognitively arrange those stimuli, and then motorically respond to them is an individual affair. It would be an injustice to assume that we are all neurologically identical. It is true that the anatomical structure and physiological functioning of the nervous system are virtually the same in everyone. One nerve impulse looks just like another — whether we see it in male or female, in child or adult, in a Sunday afternoon badminton player or a professional athlete; in the eye or the hand or the lumbosacral junction. There are fifteen thousand million of these impulses going on inside us (Eckstein 1970). The manner in which we organize these impulses, however, is a personal, individualistic affair.

Consequently, motor behavior *must* be given allowances for individualism. Everyone learns motor performances in a personal fashion. The allowances inherent in the concept of freedom must also be extended to the motor medium. Individual neurological differences must be acknowledged and permission given for each student to receive, interpret, and respond to situations within his/her own neural organizational abilities. Movement education is never show and tell from the teacher, but always allow and suggest.

THE GRANTING OF FREEDOM

It is probably safe to assume that some readers may have a genuine interest in promoting the self-appropriated learnings which are part of movement education and yet may not have done so because of the uncertainties involved. If so, a few brief suggestions can now be made. No one has researched the actual techniques for initiating a freedom-based, open-ended educational setting, although Havelock's summary (1969) of four thousand reports is worthy of reference. In the absence of true research, we are left to rely instead on opinions and empirical observations which are quite numerous. There seems to be a rather general agreement, however, on how one can most effectively establish the atmosphere of freedom necessary for discovery-type learning. Essentially, the suggestions are as follows:

1. *Give Freedom Gradually.* To generate the physical freeing essential for movement education, the environment must first permit the psychological and attitudinal freedoms which exist as states of mind. Students must *feel* free before they can respond to the dispositions of movement education. But the granting of such freedom cannot come to students as a sudden and unexpected allowance. Psychological freedom may take some time to work, particularly in situations which are presently very formalistic. In fact, if this freedom is given too abruptly, the dramatic change may result in effects which are exactly the opposite of those desired, even including student rejection of the whole idea (Hart 1970).

   Fundamentally, then, if certain constraints within the present environmeneed to be lifted for the attitude of movement education to work, they should be loosened slowly. Freedom must be given in gradually increasing allowances. And it can only be given to the degree that students are able to handle the responsibilities which are part of their new liberty.

2. *Give Freedom with Meaning.* The real intent of giving freedom is to allow students to respond more independently to learning situations. However, a reprieve from a previously disciplined environment may be interpreted by students as a license for unruly behavior. Psychological freedom is not only a fairly difficult concept to understand, it is also a difficult allowance to be simultaneously given by the teacher and received by students. It may be vulnerable to considerable misinterpretation. Consequently, to reduce the possibility of misunderstanding, the teacher must make clear to students that the new allowances have significance. For example, if certain rules, policies, or procedures are going to be altered, students should be told why these changes are being made. Such an explanation provides for a readiness to accept the modifications and greatly alleviates the risk inherent in any change (Cole 1972).

3. *Give Freedom with Feeling.* The ultimate test of the freedom is that it must be nonverbally *sensed* by students. While it is possible to explain certain ramifications of the allowances, the essence of the meaning comes through an *attitude* about the whole process. Any counterfeit attempt by the teacher will eventually result in student recognition of the insincerity. Therefore, if the establishment of an atmosphere of freedom is in opposition to the teacher's inclination the attempt may be prone to failure. The teacher cannot *pretend* that the freedom reflects some kind of inner conviction. The affair must have an air of honesty. It is not necessary (or even possible) to *tell* students about the attitude of the freedom being given; rather, it must be given without any strain by the teacher, and the impressions must be subconsciously received by students.

4. *Give Freedom with Allowance for Variability.* Providing the conditions which foster individuality requires that the teacher be able to accept the variable responses which will in fact occur. Exploratory learning generates as many different responses as there are students. Thus, while a teacher may have an ultimate objective in mind for the end product of the educational experiences, students must be accorded the liberty to arrive at that point in their own way and at their own pace.

EVALUATION BELONGS TO STUDENTS

Often, the situational problems presented to students for their exploration are open-ended in that there is no one, single, exclusively correct response. Rather, the problems permit a diversity of answers. When saying to a student, "Can you discover three ways of moving forward on the balance beam while changing your posture?" the teacher is merely asking that the student become directly involved with the problem. However, if the question were "How do you need to swing the golf club to be able to get more loft on the ball?" the situation does represent a more specific response. In the latter case the expectation is that the student will arrive (albeit by self-discovery) at the anticipated motor response.

But it does not really matter how general or specific the objectives of the movement explorations are. What always remains as part of the process is that evaluation is the responsibility of students. The teacher does not act in the traditional capacity telling students when they are right or wrong. Rather, the ability to appraise the results of a movement is expected to be acquired by the students themselves through their own experimentation. In effect, it means that students will become their own best critics.

This situation does not imply, however, that the teacher refrains from making any judgments about movement efficiency. In order to promote functionally operative motor patterns, the teacher *must* make assessments about the relative "correctness" of student responses. What changes is the manner in which such appraisals are relayed to students. For example, if a student were to say to the teacher, "I can't understand why I keep hitting my serve into the net," the teacher would not respond with a conclusive answer such as "It's because you are throwing the ball too far out in front of you." Instead, the teacher should maintain the method of student inquiry by offering possibilities: "Do you have any idea why that might be happening?" or "Do you suppose the toss of the ball could have any bearing on that?" or "Is there some way you could change your grip on the racket to overcome the tendency of the ball to go downward?" Always, the purpose is for the student to discover the answer, perhaps with the assistance of (but not dependence on) the teacher.

Such a system of evaluation is actually an obligation of any teacher who is using the principles of movement education. It would be inconsistent to ask that students experiment with and discover solutions to problems and then have an outside agency (the teacher) make all the decisions about results. In contrast, when students are granted the privilege of assessing their own responses, then the evaluative process is consistent with the teaching method. Both processes are now approached from the same frame of reference. Furthermore, since evaluations remain within the context of a problem-solving endeavor, those evaluations now become a *learning* factor. Appraisals of responses to problems are not so much a "test" of rightness or wrongness as they are a continuation of the entire problem-solving process itself. In fact, evaluation becomes so much a part of the whole affair that it is virtually indistinguishable from the actual learning. And this is a great advantage, for it is well documented (see especially Travers 1973) that any evaluative tool can best be utilized as a learning device when it supplies students with *information*. Therein is the profit of movement education — for in any problem-solving venture the learning and the evaluation occur simultaneously and are synonymous.

INFORMATION COMES FROM INSIDE

Perhaps the greatest service this holistic concept of freedom provides is in its focus of student attention. Traditional teaching methods place considerable reliance on outside sources (teachers, books, reference materials, etc.). These sources provide the initial information for learning and then evaluate how well students have acquired that information. In movement education, the sources are mostly internal. Initial learnings (the trial-and-error experimentations) are first generated from within students; then the information regarding effectiveness of responses can also become an internal factor.

The psychological freedom which surrounds (and is necessary for) a program of movement education will automatically turn students inward, at least cognitively. Additionally, we may now consider the potential source of information which exists inside all of us in a *neurological* form. This source is an underrated, and generally underused, medium for communication with our internal selves. It exists not so much in a conceptual framework as in a tangible, biological reality. We'll have a look at it now.

THE NERVE
OF IT ALL

A NEURAL SERVANT OR A NERVOUS HINDRANCE

There is an area of your brain called the *reticular formation* which is responsible for all sensitive behavior. When you fold your hands together behind your head as you watch TV, you have essentially covered the area of its location. What is important is not so much where it is as what it does.

The reticular formation receives information from all sense systems — sounds and sights and smells and tastes and feelings. Even thoughts. All come into the reticular formation and are scrutinized relative to their importance. Every piece of information — all of which exists inside us in the form of nerve impulses — gets appraised. The reticular formation, without our having to think about it, decides what information should be brought to our conscious attention and what should be discarded.

It does its job rather well, normally. As a great service to us, it filters out much irrelevant daily input. It saves us the bother of clouding our brains with information which has no meaning at the moment. Thus we can go to a movie on Saturday night when we are tired, our back is sunburned, the seat is too cramped, the tickets cost too much, and we really ought to be at home working on income tax. But never mind all that — we can enjoy the show anyhow because our reticular formation says to forget it — it isn't relevant to our enjoying the entertainment. The reticular formation has a more difficult time, however, in a golf game when we might score below a 90 for the first time ever and a friend helplessly wants our putt to drop. That is relevant information. Putting a golf ball is far more active and difficult than watching a movie. So here we are, having to do something. A great many impulses are coming in at the moment; so many, in fact, that the reticular formation cannot handle all of them — the other players, the sounds, the feel of the club, the score. All this information is transformed into nerve impulses, and nerve impulses are energy. The reticular formation has a limit, however. It can manage only so much energy; when there is more than its limit, it cannot deal with the excess energy. So it does the only thing it can do — it turns away the excess. The stockpiles are full, it says. No more room for anymore nerve impulses. But energy is energy. It can't be made to simply disappear. It has to go somewhere. Therefore, when the reticular formation cannot handle this nervous energy, the excess "spills over" into the rest of the body. For a reason that no one really knows, the excess energy goes into the muscular system — to every muscle in the body, to those which we need to execute the putting stroke and also to those which fight against that execution. When this extra "spilled-over" energy enters the muscles, it does what all nerve impulses do to muscles. It makes them contract, not very much, but enough to make the putter feel heavy and the stroke feel awkward. We quite literally get in our own way. Not because we want to, but because the reticular formation, which serves us so well when there is no stress, has now become incapable of standing up to the pressure.

IT'S THE SAME FOR EVERYONE

All people have the same neurological foundation. The reticular formation performs the same service for all. Every reticular formation in every person has a saturation point beyond which it will refuse to accept any more information. The difference from person to person is in where that saturation point is reached. It is high for some, low for others, in the middle for most of us. Professional athletes generally can receive a great amount of input before any spills over, which is one of the reasons they are professional athletes. They are able to execute well under pressure. The majority of us, however, are given only average capabilities for handling input — at least when it comes to the performance of a motor skill. We "tighten up" at a lower level of input than the people whom we are willing to pay to watch hit a ball or kick a ball or put a ball through a metal hoop.

Now, then, let's assume a student in your tennis class is having trouble with the backhand. Hit after hit is erratic. Any ball that manages to cross the net is a chance occurrence, and any ball that goes into the opposing court is almost an accident. Your student is becoming frustrated. In this situation you probably do what most conscientious teachers would do — you *teach*. At least, you try to teach. If nothing else, you supply the student with information which you hope will be helpful: "Turn your shoulders more." "Keep your elbow close to you in the backswing." "Shift your weight to your front foot as you hit." "Swing through the ball." While this terminology may mean something to you, it may mean *nothing* to the student. Further, the more difficulty the student has, the more you may feel obliged to offer additional information.

TEACHING BETTER BY SAYING LESS

Unfortunately, we probably all make that same mistake now and then. After all, we are employed to teach, and when nothing seems to be happening (that is, no progress in learning seems to be taking place), we sense a professional obligation to try to *make* something happen. But in the process, we may actually hinder learning. We may *think* we are doing what we should be doing, but in reality we may be overloading the reticular formation with too much input. Everything we say to a student is converted into energy, in the form of nerve impulses. The more we say, the more energy there is; and the more energy, the more likely that it will go beyond the point of saturation for the particular student.

In fact, what we should often do is *decrease* the amount of information offered students. The tennis player who is having difficulty with the backhand already has some self-originated energy coming from the stress of the frustration. This is an especially hindering factor in tennis, which by its nature is a motor activity requiring relatively controlled relaxation for efficient execution. No one can physiologically fight her/himself, muscle against muscle, and hit a well-stroked backhand.

Realistically, most motor performance demands a similar regulation. When we ski, we cannot resist the hill. Instead, we must more or less "flow with the terrain," adjusting our responses to the constant changes. The same body attitude of adjusted relaxation is needed to play golf or swim or to bowl or to play badminton. The body must be fluid because we need rhythmical movements. And if *we* who are adults need such movements, we can imagine the needs of a child who is, say, about to make a first try at a leg circle on a high bar. Certainly the child does not need an overload of information: "Throw your head and shoulders forward as you start." "Kick your leg backward." "Stretch out at first, then tuck as you get halfway around." It would be easy to overdo. There is already plenty of nervous energy in the reticular formation. Maybe all we should say at this time is "Make sure you hang on to the bar."

The real meaning of physical freeing, then, consists in not overloading the reticular formation with too much input. When we impose too much information on students, we are constricting their movement potentials. By giving smaller amounts of input (at least in the sense of providing less static information), we allow the muscular system of students to be more free — less hindered by an overabundance of subconscious nervous energy. This is the very direct principle of movement education: Never *tell* students the things they *must* do, instead merely suggest. The effect is to relieve the atmosphere of overwhelming demands and substitute a freedom which removes the pressure.

LEARNING TO READ BODY SIGNALS

We've freed the mind. We've freed the body. We've provided psychological freedom so that students may *feel* they are at complete liberty to try their own ways of performing. And we've given a physical freeing to prevent an overloading of the reticular formation. Now, in addition, we will try to help students become more consciously in contact with the information available to them through their own senses.

We're back to the mind-body relation again. First, we need to *relieve* the mind to free the body. Now, we can *alert* the mind to what the body is saying. First, there's an allowance; then, listening.

The process works like biofeedback. Biofeedback is a revolutionary but essentially simple concept which can be used as an effective way of harmonizing the mind with the body. Broadly seen, feedback of any kind is sensory information which usually results from some kind of response. Basically, it is the "feeding back" of biological information to any person whose body is producing that information in the first place, a return of some input from an output. If we hit a thumb with a hammer, there's feedback. If we grope for a light switch in the dark, feedback tells us when we find it. If we raise an arm behind the head to throw a ball, feedback tells us where the arm is.

All muscular activity involves a biofeedback circuitry; it is generally referred to, however, as *kinesthetic feedback*. This activity could be viewed as electrochemical energy generated from muscle movement and then sent on to the reticular formation as nerve impulses. Even muscles at rest send out small volleys of nerve impulses. But this communication of movement to the brain

39

is so ordinary that we never really think too much about it. We need not think about how we tie our shoes in the morning, put on the coffee, pour the orange juice, and walk to the car. These movements are the result of an automatic system.

The real drama of the kinesthetic feedback system, however, is that we *can* tune in to our inner senses. We could probably tie our shoes blindfolded, but to do that we would need to give conscious attention to what the receptors in our fingers are telling us. Or we could deliberatively listen to the news supplied by our sensors when swinging a driver, or trying a front turnover on the trampoline, or tossing a few darts at the local pub. Normally, we rely on the reticular formation to *filter out* most of the stimuli received during the day. Since much of the kinesthetic information received is not necessary for functioning, we ignore it. But the real value of the process is that we can also override the reticular formation and *focus in* on some of the information which may be to our benefit.

As we learn to monitor our internal being, we become more familiar with it; with practice we can also learn to *control* it. We can get inside a muscle, learn to perceive it directly, read its activity, and then influence it. For example, in a very direct application of this fact, we can readily experience the differences felt from changes in muscular tension. In a technique first developed by Jacobson (1957), countless numbers of people have learned simple ways to relax their bodies. It operates on the principle that one must first recognize *differences* in tension. To do so one must produce those differences. Thus, according to the technique, one is asked to create a tense state by, say, clenching the fist as hard as one can and then letting the mind try to *feel* the tension, focusing fully on the sensation. Then one allows the hand to relax completely, again playing the mind on the feedback which comes from a state of relaxation. But most importantly, one is asked also to recognize the *differences* in the feelings. Next, one clenches the fist half as hard as before, again recognizing the change in tension. This process continues, using all other parts of the body until the differences in sensations are fully perceived. In the final act of this scheme one becomes capable of voluntarily *producing* selected sensations. The theory is that since the brain now *knows* what the sensation of relaxation feels like, one can now *create* it. Thus, when one lies down at night and the body is still humming from the events of the day, all that is necessary for relaxation is to allow the brain to establish a state that it already knows.

This procedure is a deceptively simple way of identifying the feelings we have inside us. Feedback gives us continuous, accurate indicators of internal affairs. We can learn to use this information not only to help us fall asleep at night, but also to get rid of that persistent slice, or to return the ball over the net, or to do the twisting dive that we haven't done for years at Friday night's swim party. For students, this technique is one of the most personal ways for them to come to know themselves. Such knowing is a very real internal sensing of one's own person.

In the literature, the kinesthetic sense is sometimes referred to as a quality of "just noticeable differences." Specifically, it means the ability of a person to perceive small differences in sensory feedback. For example, suppose you were to pick up a ten pound weight. How much additional weight would need to be added before you would notice the increase? Only an ounce? A few ounces? Another full pound? While almost everyone would be able to recognize the difference between ten pounds and eleven pounds, not many persons could sense a difference between ten pounds and ten pounds, two ounces. Those who could would be said to have a very exacting perception of just noticeable differences. The same neurological functioning allows a highly skilled golfer to make minor variations in swing to compensate for deviant ball flight, or a gymnast to make midair corrections in performance, or a baseball catcher to receive a fluttering knuckleball. Its operation is similar to that of a heat-sensing rocket travelling on a direct line toward a target. When the rocket strays off-line slightly, an electrical feedback circuit within makes the corrections necessary to get it back on its direct path toward the target.

Within each person the kinesthetic sense — the ability to recognize just noticeable differences — is an individual and variable quality with which each person was born. Some persons quite simply have a more refined system than others. In that respect, one point should be made perfectly clear: In no way can we expect a program of movement education, or any other system which focuses on internal feedback, to develop a more precise operation of nervous transmission. The kinesthetic feedback system with which we were born is ours forever. Like most other biological systems of the body, we can do absolutely nothing to enhance its basic functioning (Singer 1975). Thus we cannot anticipate that movement education will hone the kinesthetic sense of students. We are all what we are, and we always shall be.

On the other hand, we *can* become more alert to the feedback we receive. We can become better listeners to our own signals. Both the Jacobson relaxation technique and biofeedback training accomplish this objective. No useless attempt is made to develop something which is innately predetermined. Instead, what is possible is to learn to depend more on information that is available to us. The effect is no different from what

41

happens when a person loses the sense of sight. The sense of hearing, despite popular opinion, does *not* become more acute. Rather, the person becomes more dependent on sound for the information which previously had come from sight. The sounds now heard had always been heard before but were never really tuned in to. There is simply a change of attentiveness, not a refinement in the auditory sense.

So it is with movement education. There is no hope for developing an increased efficiency of electrochemical events. Rather, the objective is to give attention to the kinesthetic feedback that is always available but is usually ignored.

THE INTERNALIZATION OF LEARNING

Actually, it was all Rudolph Laban's doing. Laban was born in Germany and spent his early life in that country. When his ideas were not well received there, he found solace in England where he became the pioneer of movement education.

Laban believed that physical movement could be an expression of life itself. He considered it most viable means for discovering one's self and one's existence with the world. Human beings, he said, were "total" only when they were moving. The multiple variables of thought, feeling, and will could only be combined in a movement medium.

No one understood movement education at first. Many people thought it was just another name for modern dance, which it was not. Others saw it as merely another way to teach gymnastics, which it was originally. The early confusion came from misinterpretations of Laban's ideas. Some of his writings (see especially Laban 1948 and 1960) have great existentialistic overtones and often do remind one of modern dance. Further, the provisions for learning which are characteristic of movement education are readily applied through gymnastics. It has taken some time to apprehend the real meaning of what Laban was telling us. It appears that he was actually speaking about the reticular formation, as well as about kinesthesis and biofeedback — not in the same terminology or even the same thought, but in substance.

FOUR DIMENSIONS OF MOVEMENT

Laban analyzed movement from the standpoint of certain principles, only four of which he believed warranted attention: *space, weight, time,* and *flow.* Laban regarded all movement as a blending, in various degrees, of these four qualities. Descriptively, they are as follows:

1. *Space.* Essentially, this quality refers to the manner in which movement uses an area. Laban first thought of it as either an economic quality of "personal space," which is that area within reach of an individual; or the more expansive consideration of "general space," which is everywhere else. Additionally, the body can move in space in different directions, in different pathways, at different levels, or in different shapes. Thus, the baseball pitcher contorts into a series of movements within the realm of personal space, and the batter who hits and runs and slides is using general space with all its variances.

2. *Weight.* As the term might imply, this quality is the degree of muscular tension involved in movement. It may be strong, resistant, and forceful; or it may be relaxed, light, and easy. When you chop firewood on Saturday morning, you use movements of different weight from those used when you play golf that afternoon.

3. *Time.* This is a quality of tempo. A movement can be slow or fast. This factor also includes the amplitudes of being sudden and abbreviated or progressive and sustained. The speed of movement can also change throughout, becoming faster or slower. A tennis forehand normally involves a movement which increases in impulse as the ball is hit, although it could also be intentionally slowed. Moreover, the time of a movement can be a series of rhythmical changes, as is so true in dance.

4. *Flow.* This is the aspect of the fluency of movement. It may be "bound," meaning movement which can be stopped and held without much difficulty, as in many wrestling maneuvers; or it may be a flailing abandon, as in the gyrations of a discus thrower.

The important feature of all these qualities is not so much the definitions or differences but the fact that differences in movement dimensions exist. Laban realized this fact. He was simply trying to delineate the variables and give direction to teaching. Over the years Laban's ideas have often been misunderstood, misjudged, fanaticized, overestimated, underestimated, and otherwise maligned. His main objective was to make us aware that learners move in various dimensions and that the essence of teaching and self-appropriated learning is to attend to all the variables.

FROM INNER SPACE TO OUTER SPACE

Some authors have considered these variables as the foundation of a program of "basic movement." From this point of view, efficiency of movement is assumed to develop from an initial learning of the how, what, and where of motor activity. A kinesthetic recognition and voluntary control of changes serve as the motoric ground floor for later refinement of movement patterns. The contention is that learners need to enhance (or recapture) the natural biological relations between the proprioceptive sense and the cognitive awareness of it. Consequently, in a designed program of movement education, the first experiences are oriented toward a stimulus of the basic differences in movement qualities. This procedure is very similar in context to Jacobson's method of teaching relaxation.

The teacher of such basic movement awareness may wish to select an organizational theme and give most of the attention to the theme during classes. For example, a sample lesson for the concept of space for children might proceed somewhat like the following illustration which is an adaptation of lessons suggested by Gilliom (1970, pp. 54–60):

Begin by having the children seated on the floor, each child in an area where s/he cannot reach out and touch another. The first series of explorations do not require children to move away from their areas. The verbalizations given are merely suggestive of movements to be evoked and are not to be taken as absolutes or complete possibilities.

1. Move one hand around you, reaching as many places as you can.

2. Now, move the other hand around. Can you find some space with this hand that you cannot find with your other one?

3. Move both hands around, finding as much of your own space as you can. Is there space near you? far away? as much in back of you as in front?

4. Now, move only your head. Does your head move in the same way as your hands? Can you move your head to as many places as you could move your hands? Can you use the rest of your body to help you move your head, while still staying seated?

5. Now, let's all try moving just one foot around. Move it into as much space as you can. Can you take it as many places as you could take your hands? How can you move your foot around you without touching the floor? Can you get it high above you? Now, try all these things with your other foot.

6. Here's a strange one. Put your head on the floor, and see how many places you can move the rest of your body.

7. Now, you will need to listen carefully, because there will be some changes for you to make without stopping any of your movements. Start by moving one hand around you again, as you did before. Now, move the other hand so that both hands are moving. Stretch as far as you can without getting up. Can you make it seem as if you are touching a lot of space around you? And now, make your two hands go in two different directions at the same time. Can one hand go in straight lines while the other goes in circles? Keep your hands moving and, now, move your head at the same time. Can you add one foot to all this movement? And, then, the other foot? Are you moving as many parts of you as you can into as many places as you can?

In these early movement explorations, sufficient time must be provided for each student to experience each of the suggestions. Taking too much time between the verbal stimuli is preferable to taking too little, particularly since the time interval may actually allow for some cognitive perceptions of the movements.

Also, it is good to circulate among students while giving the verbalizations since it may be necessary to make individual suggestions here and there to those having difficulty inventing changes in their movement patterns.

8. Now, put both hands on the floor and see how many ways you can move your body around your hands. Keep both hands glued to the floor all the time. Can you get your feet very close to your hands? very far away? Can you get one of your feet above you? both feet?

9. Now, lie on your back. Can you try some of the same movements? Touch your hands to your feet. Now, get them as far away from each other as you can. Roll over to lie on your stomach. Can you reach your hands or feet into the space that is now above you? Is this the same space that is behind you when you are standing?

10. Now, stand up. Keep one foot on the ground, as if it were nailed there, and use all parts of your body to find and reach

into all the space around you. Can you reach into high space? low space? Can you twist your body around to touch the space that is behind you?

11. Touch the floor, now, with both feet and one hand. Reach all around your space. Is it smaller than it was before? Touch only one foot and one hand to the floor. How does this change your movements? Try balancing on one foot, and then reach all around you, high, low, and to the sides. Put both your knees on the floor and do the same thing. Now, use any two parts of your body that you haven't used before to support your weight. Use two different parts this time. Now, use only one part of your body to support your weight. Use a body part other than your feet. Can you use one body part that you haven't used before?

This beginning motor experimentation is intended to generate an initial kinesthetic sensitivity to the basic changes and possibilities of bodily movements in space. As is true with all nonstructured problems, the movement responses may be quite varied, and all the variances could be correct. This is simply a result of the fact that open-ended suggestion are subject to diverse interpretations. For example, if the children are lying on their backs and the suggestion is given to "reach your arms high," some students may extend their arms upward toward the ceiling, while others may stretch their arms beyond the top of their heads, parallel with the floor. Both responses are acceptable in the minds of students.

What is more important than individual interpretations of any single problem is the *variability* that each student can demonstrate. All students should be able to execute a number of different ways of accomplishing the same end. And they should be able to alter the responses at will with a full recognition of whether or not they have previously used a particular pattern. The simple suggestion "Now, do it a different way" should evoke a new response for the same problem from each of the students. Some may not be able to make such distinctions and instead will persist in movement patterns which resemble previous ones. In this case, if further verbal suggestions do not seem to elicit varied responses, it may be well to have these students watch others, not for the purpose of imitation but to give them a visual suggestion to go along with the auditory input they have already received.

Next, students can move into a more general utilization of space.

12. Now, we are going to use the big space that is all around you in this room (or a defined area outside). Let's all move around in

this big space, going to all parts of it. Try to keep away from everyone else as you move around. How many different ways can you move through this space? Try something different from running. Can you move backward? sideways? fast? slow? high? low?

13. See if you can get your feet very high as you move. How high can you get your whole body? Is there something you can do with your arms to help you get your whole body into the air? Can your knees be higher than your hips when you are in the air? Are there different things you can do when in the air?

14. Try to be in a stretched position as you move around the room. Now, be very small as you move. Can you move by using your hands and feet together on the floor? Can you go from one place to another by having both feet land on the floor at the same time? And here's a difficult one — can you move around from one place to another without touching your feet or hands to the floor?

Students should be using all the space, not just part of it. Again, there should be a versatility shown by each of the students. Sometimes it may be helpful to have half the class observe the other half, or one student who is particularly inventive might be asked to show the movement possibilities to the entire class.

To add another dimension, children could be asked to "freeze" into a static position on a given signal (a word or clap of hands). This variation offers them a chance to have a "stop-action" still photograph of the patterns they are executing — a visual representation of their actions. Thus, they can inspect their responses and gain additional information regarding their production of movement.

THE BACKSIDE OF THE FOREHAND

Do these exploratory experiences have meaning only for children? Does everything end there, with no further implications other than the experience itself?

Every spring on tennis courts all over the country, there are conversations similar to the following:

TEACHER: Sandy, you know you're taking your racket back awfully far every time you hit a forehand. Do you know what that is often doing to the direction of your hit?

SANDY: I'm not sure what you mean.

47

TEACHER: Well, have you noticed how many times the ball goes off to your right?

SANDY: Actually, I have. In fact, I've noticed that it happens when the ball comes to me very fast. I don't seem to get the racket around to return the ball.

TEACHER: Yes, that's right. But I think you could remedy that by taking a shorter backswing. Do you know how that would help?

SANDY: I think so. It would take less time.

TEACHER: Exactly. As it is now, your backswing is taking a lot of time because it is so big, and you don't have that kind of time when the ball is coming fast. As a result, you are hitting the ball late and it's kicking off to your right.

SANDY: I'm embarrassed that I haven't learned that by this time. Other people have also told me about it. I just don't seem to be able to do anything to correct it.

TEACHER: Give it a try. See if you can hit the next few forehands with an abbreviated backswing.

(But the next several swings produce the same lengthy backswing.)

SANDY: Is that any better?

TEACHER: It's still going back pretty far. Can you shorten it?

SANDY: I thought I was.

TEACHER: Well, not really. Let's have a look at it — take your racket back about as far as you would if you were going to hit a forehand and hold it there. See — it's going around behind you almost a full half circle away from the point at which you hit the ball.

SANDY: Yes, I see what you are saying. I mean, I can *see* it, but I can't seem to *feel* it when I'm hitting.

Within the dynamics of any motor execution there is always a spatial component. Something is moving somewhere, in space. And frequently, in sports skills, the movement patterns are executed out of the visual field. It is not possible to visually inspect the arms as they crank up to hit a golf ball, or to see how a bowling ball is being swung during the approach, or to watch the racket move into the backswing. Instead, the positions in space must be *sensed*.

48

To move in space requires that one first become aware of it. There is *up* space, *down* space, *front* space, *back* space, *left* space, and *right* space. The performer must be able to know the "whereness" of the spatial world and how the body moves in it.

As it happens, *back* space — that area which is behind or in back of someone — is the least well recognized of all spatial coordinates (Barsch 1968). It is probably the last of the segments of space to become developmentally organized and cognitively distinguished; that is, in the normal sequential development of childhood maturation, back space takes a back seat. A young child spends a great deal of time in generating a spatial awareness, but the acquisition of this sense is largely oriented to front space. Back space seems lost in the haste for maturity. Still, there is no question of its significance in the later development of movement efficiency. An awareness of back space (1) allows an individual to localize stimuli which are occurring behind that person, (2) permits the evaluation of events in back space without the need to forsake what is happening in front space, (3) provides a consciousness of body movements in back space without any necessity for visual checking, and (4) therefore places a reliance on the proprioceptive sense for information.

When a tennis ball is on its way, the event occurs in front space. But to hit the ball effectively, there must be an event that happens in back space. The skillful operation of the back space event is predicated on a kinesthetic awareness of that spatial dimension. Furthermore, the movements in back space must be purposefully altered as events change in front space. Sometimes the ball comes fast, sometimes slowly. It can come to either side or high or low or directly at a player. The execution of a single, unalterable backswing will produce only ineffective returns.

Accordingly, a movement education theme of spatial orientation should perhaps pay particular attention to back space learnings. Activities may range from a simple suggestion to "reach back and touch the space behind you" to more delineated movements whereby students might, for example, be asked to move their limbs (out of their visual fields) to a certain angle or to trace a certain pattern in the air. A critical concern in such experiences is the teacher's ability to recognize any individuals who never realize the full use of space in their responses (i.e., all space, but especially back space). Some children, when asked to find their own back space, may never actually do so. They may instead tend to keep their limbs in their fields of view, or they may reach back only partially and always in the same position. In other instances, when asked, say, to reach as high as they can (without looking at their arms), some children may extend their

49

arms only partially or may not reach directly upward. In their own minds, they may *think* they are reaching as high as they can, but upon visual inspection they are often surprised to find that indeed they are not. This is a matter of mind overruling the information which is available through the kinesthetic sense. To circumvent this possibility, the learning of spatial awareness should often take the sequence of first performing a movement without visual feedback (either out of the visual field or with the eyes closed), followed by a visual "checking" of the movement. In this way, the learner's reliance for information is directed toward the kinesthetic sense. The anticipation is that the learner's receptivity to that information will increase and the final product will be a heightening of the ability to make judgments about and changes within the movements which occur in back space.

A WELL-BALANCED PERSON

The execution of all movement is, of course, multidimensional. Tossing a few basketballs through the rim down at the recreation center, for example, is not just a spatial matter. The coordination of all the factors of movement is involved.

One of the more significant components of motor efficiency is that of balance. This is not to say that balance is more important than the other components — but it does seem to be an integral part of all movement. Although Laban did not consider balance independently, this element runs constantly throughout his writing. It is given specific attention here because it can so readily be included in the learning of the other dimensions of movement and because it seems particularly well aligned with spatial orientation.

Balance can be interpreted as any held position. From this point of view, it could be attended to by suggesting to students the execution of the following exercises:

Any balance using a wide base

Any balance using a narrow base

A balance with the body facing upward

A balance with the body facing downward

A bridge-shaped balance

A balance using any other body shape (straight, round, etc.)

Balancing on different body parts

Balancing with different body parts as the highest point

Balancing objects in the hand, on the shoulder, on the knee, etc.

Balancing objects while changing body positions as in the preceding examples.

These activities are only a beginning, however. Holding balanced positions statically does not represent the learning increments which are important for efficient movement. The real world of balance is more dynamic. Very few movement skills require prolonged static positions of held balance. The movement education program should therefore more frequently create a series of "gravitational encounters" which will offer students problems of active balance. To assist in this endeavor, it is often feasible to reduce the normal base of support by asking students to perform movements on a balance beam, on ordinary benches, on boxes, on a rope laid on the floor, or on a simple chalk line drawn on the floor.

Here is an example of a sequence of activities that could be used on a balance beam. It could be easily adapted to another narrow support medium. This first sequence presented is relatively structured and offered here as potential activities around which suggestive explorations can be built.

1. Walk forward on the beam, arms out to the side, and then backward, arms out to the side.

   (Here already we have the confrontation with back space again. When asked to walk backward on a balance beam, many students will turn their heads to see where they are going. But the "knowing" of back space can only be developed without continual dependence on visual feedback. Consequently, students must be encouraged to perform movements in back space by keeping the head forward.)

2. Walk to the middle of the beam, then turn and walk backward the rest of the way.

3. Walk forward with hands on hips, then backward with hands on hips.

4. Walk forward balancing an object on the head (book, bean bag, cardboard square), then backward.

5. Walk forward and pick up an object laid on the beam, place it on top of the head, and continue to the end of the beam.

6. Walk over or around obstacles placed on the beam (ropes, books, etc.).

7. Go under an obstacle (a rope, other students' outstretched arms, etc.) forward and backward.

8. Walk backward with hands clasped behind the body.

9. Walk forward and backward, balancing objects in the hands.

10. Walk sideward, left foot leading, then right foot, first without crossover steps, then with crossover steps.

11. Walk to the middle of the beam, lower your center of gravity (touch one knee to the beam, touch hands to the beam, etc.), then rise and continue. Repeat walking backward.

12. Hop the length of the beam on the right foot, then on the left foot; then alternate.

13. Go to the middle of the beam, balance on one foot and turn around, continue backward to the end of the beam. Use the other foot to balance and turn next time.

14. Walk to the middle of the beam, pick up an object laid on the beam, place it behind you on the beam, and continue on.

15. Hold a wand or stick in the hands, walk forward, step over the wand while keeping the hands on it, then continue. Repeat walking backward.

16. Walk forward and backward, keeping eyes fixed on an object (a spot on the wall, the ceiling, etc.).

17. Walk forward and backward, keeping eyes fixed on a moving object (another person moving, the teacher swinging an object on a rope, etc.).

18. Walk forward, backward, sideward, any other movement, with eyes closed.

19. Two persons start at opposite ends, pass each other on the beam, continue on.

20. Move forward and backward on all fours.

With a little invention, a multitude of other movements could be added to those listed. However, in their context, attention is directly given to the kinesthetic sense. Exploratory problem solving might be added to these experiences by giving students on the beam suggestions such as the following (adapted from Mosston 1966, pp. 202–7):

1. Assume any position you want on the beam. Which parts of your body will disrupt your balance if you make only a small movement of them? Are there parts which have less effect on your balance when you move them? Why?

2. What happens if you move a body part forward? Does it upset your balance less than if you move it sideward? Can you change the manner in which you are using your base of support to give

you more balance? Does this change give you better support when you move a body part forward or backward?

3. Move a body part to the side. What can you do on the other side of your body to maintain your balance? Is there a relationship between the two body parts you just moved to either side?

4. Now, try the three preceding activities while moving forward on the beam. Does your forward motion change any of the effects? Try the same movements going backward.

5. Choose any body position on the beam, and discover what kinds of motion can be initiated from that position.

6. Select another body position as a start, and try the same motions from that position. Do there seem to be better starting positions for initiating certain movements?

7. Move along the beam in any way that you like, changing your level from high to low to high, etc., as you move.

8. Do the same movements by going in a different way (backward, sideward, etc.).

9. Can you move along the beam using two body parts other than your feet to give you support?

10. Can you move across the beam with a series of stop-and-go movements?

11. Move forward in any way that you like, make a complete turn in the middle, and continue on. Then come back and do another turn, this time with a lower center of gravity. Which of the turns is more efficient?

12. Can you add the movement of any other body part while you turn?

13. Experiment to find out the least amount of base you need to support yourself as you move along the beam.

14. Now, find the largest amount of base you can to support yourself.

15. Try different sizes and kinds of supports, and see which ones seem to give you the best ability to stop and go quickly. Why are some better than others?

16. As you move forward on the beam, can you change your posture into something shorter? taller? longer? a round shape? something straight? very low? Try all these postures again, this time moving backward, then sideways.

17. Keep your arms very close to you as you move forward and backward. Then keep them as far away from you as you can. Which position gives you more balance? Why? Is there another position in which you can hold your arms which is even better than these two?

18. Close your eyes and move forward on the beam. Can you feel how your arms are helping to keep your balance?

19. Keep your eyes closed, and move your arms around in different positions. Can you tell when your arms are in the best position for balance? How do you know?

20. Now, move around on the beam in any way that you like — forward, backward, sideways — and move all your other body parts. Keep your eyes closed all the time, and try to feel how your body can both upset and help your balance.

The underlying purpose of these experiences is to provide students with an increased sensory awareness of the interplay of balance in efficient movement. This universal concept can be generated by having students perform exploratory movements on the floor without any equipment. The examples which follow are adapted from Gilliom (1970, pp. 150–57).

1. Find a personal space where you are out of the reach of anyone.

2. Make any shape you wish and hold it as still as you can. Do you feel as if you are well balanced? Look at your base of support. What happens if you make it bigger? then smaller? Lean your body until you lose your balance. Try the same exercise with different sizes of support. Why do you lose your balance quicker with one base of support than with the others?

3. Now, try to see how many different ways you can balance yourself. Try many different body parts for your base of support. Try using one, two, three, or more body parts at the same time. See how many different shapes you can get your body into and still keep your balance.

   (Some students may have difficulty with this exploration. Inventiveness sometimes needs a little external help. Hence, as before, individual suggestions given by the teacher are often beneficial. Or the whole class could occasionally watch other students who are particularly imaginative.)

4. Now, move around the room. Try changing directions quickly. Can you do anything to help change direction? Try lowering your center of gravity and see if that makes any difference.

54

5. Now, stop and take a position which would help you to stay on balance if someone pushed you from the front. Look at your base of support. Why are you standing that way? Would it change if someone were to push you from the side? from the back?

6. Now, take a position which you believe would help you to get a fast start for running forward. Then run out of that position a little way. Try another starting position and compare.

   (As these explorations proceed, it is good to frequently call for the students to "freeze" for a few seconds so that the base of support and the direction of impulse can be identified.)

7. Now, take a wide stance. Lean your body forward until you go off balance. This time let your weight go toward the floor and catch it with your hands. How can the arms absorb the shock?

   (A number of experiences should be provided in which students are asked to intentionally let their weight go off balance. Such experiences encourage confidence and recognition that they can still operate in an off-balance position.)

8. With a wide stance, put your hands on the floor in front of you, weight on all fours. Hold that position for a few seconds. Then put your head down, chin close to your chest. Let your weight go over your head, onto your hands, and roll out. Try to recover a balance position as you finish your roll. (If available, mats ease the effect of inefficient performances.)

9. Put your head and both hands on the mat. (Use a towel to support the head if no mats are available.) Think about how you can place these three body parts to give you the best support. Now, try to get one foot above the rest of your body, then both feet. Get them as high as you can.

10. Now, let's all walk around the room. Stay away from everyone else. When you see someone else in front of you, change your direction. Everyone move in slow motion. Can you tell what you are doing to change direction? How is your body doing this? Now, go back to walking again. Keep changing direction to avoid bumping into other people. Now, let's go at a slow run. Do you need to do anything differently to change direction? And now, run faster. Can you still avoid everyone else? Must you do anything differently when running fast?

THE INSIDE OF THE INFIELD

In the dynamic world of sports, balance is a constant; that is, it is constantly present and always a part of performance. Presumably, balance is

55

also something that we learned a long time ago and therefore does not need much attention now. We learned to walk, run, jump off a fence, ride a bike, and generally we seem to be in rather decent control of our own balance. Yet, on any public tennis court we can find persons who seem to be unaware of some basic laws of balance control. It could be, perhaps, that we have sufficient command for normal everyday activities, but not enough for the extraordinary requirements of a tennis match. Or maybe the balance is there, but we just don't quite know how to use it.

We might bring some attention to the use of balance through the learning of sports skills. Assume that we are observing a junior high school class about to practice some softball fundamentals of infield play.

TEACHER: Now, then, when you are playing in the infield, what direction do you think you usually need to move to get to a batted ball?

JERRY: Well, often the ball is right in front of you, but it could be coming from any direction. Sometimes the ball is hit over your head.

TEACHER: That's true. So, if we really think about the possibilities, it means that we would need to be ready to move in any direction, because we don't know where the ball will be hit. How, then, should we take a ready stance?

SUE: You should spread your feet and be ready to go in any direction you need to go.

TEACHER: Yes, that's one thing we need to do. And when you do that, what does it do to your center of gravity?

BOB: It lowers it.

TEACHER: Exactly. You remember that we talked about that before. A lower center of gravity will help you to move more quickly. Is there anything else we should do?

CONNIE: Bend the knees and lean forward.

TEACHER: That seems logical. We should bend the knees because that will also lower our center of gravity, and it kind of sets us to spring out of our stance. But if we lean forward, it will mean we are not ready for a ball that is hit over our head. Let's all have a little experiment on this point. Find a space where you can be out of everyone's way. Now take a stance which you believe

56

gets you ready for a ball hit in any direction. After you do that, pretend that you are going after a ball and see if you can move quickly from your stance in the direction of the imaginary ball. Try all different directions.

(A few minutes are allowed for the exercise.)

TEACHER: How do you feel about it?

DAVID: I have trouble going backward.

MICHELE: I think you could bend your knees too much. And spread your feet too far.

TEACHER: You're absolutely right. Let's consider those things. Take your ready stance again. Now look around. There are a lot of different stances being shown here. Stan has his feet really wide apart.

STAN: Yes, I think they are too far.

TEACHER: It seems there may be a best way. How far apart do you think the feet should be spread?

DONNICA: How about like this?

TEACHER: I think that may be about right. They are just far enough apart so that if you could do it, you could get your shoulders in between your feet. Let's all try that distance. And now what about the rest of the body? How should we get the rest of us ready?

BARRY: You need to be on your toes.

JOANNE: And be kind of bent over.

TEACHER: Yes, that's good. It's very much like the way we begin to sit down in a chair. Try it. Everyone pretend you have a chair behind you and you are going to sit in it. But only make the first move and stop yourself after you have sat down just a couple of inches from your standing position. Does that feel about right? Bounce up and down a little, and feel the energy that could come out of that stance.

BOB: My dad always told me an infielder should be ready to go forward, and this stance makes me feel as if I can't be ready to do that.

TEACHER: Well, you have a point. You see, if you were playing third base, many times you need to move quickly

57

forward because the batter might bunt the ball. But if you were playing shortstop, you would not be going after bunts. So it seems that there may be a stance that is best for a third base player and a slightly different stance that is best for a shortstop. Let's see if we can discover the differences. . . .

In these learnings it is important not only to show the basic principles of balance, but also to demonstrate that it is sometimes advantageous to be intentionally *off* balance (e.g., when initiating a move from a stationary position). To this end students could help each other by acting as partners and playing give-and-take games where they try to upset the partner's balance; or one partner could offer some resistance to the other who is trying to move in a certain direction (for example, pushing against the lead shoulder of a partner who is attempting to move sideways).

With older students the laws of equilibrium might be explained so that they can better understand their application. For instance, if a basketball player recognizes the reasons why a pivotal move could be executed more quickly by using the ball to generate momentum, or by dropping the shoulder, or by putting the lead knee in a certain position, etc., the principles are more likely to become ingrained as normal operational routine. In fact, research evidence shows that when learners understand the mechanical principles of motor performance, their knowledge contributes to their execution of the motor acts (see especially Singer 1975).

A HEAVY MATTER

Laban's original movement qualities of weight, time, and flow are often considered separately. They are so complementary to each other, however, that they can be readily incorporated in a movement education scheme. Nonetheless, the possibility or value of isolating attention to their properties in the total program should not be ignored. They are condensed here for illustration, not necessarily as a recommendation.

There are certain movements that all professional tennis players have in common. One is to swing the racket with an accelerating velocity as they hit the ball, i.e., at the moment the racket meets the ball its speed is increasing rather than maintaining the impetus or slowing down. This is a matter of force which is an apparently uncommon feature in the swings of inexperienced players.

How does one ever learn to make this technique a standard feature of the forehand and backhand? Certainly not by listening to a teacher say over and over that we should "hit through the ball." That statement doesn't seem to make much sense unless we know exactly what it means and — even more importantly — what it *feels* like. More logically, this ability to generate and control an increasing velocity in a tennis swing should have become a preliminary part of our kinesthetic system a long time ago. Perhaps a class involved in explorations like the following might have developed such ability.

1. Some of the things I'm going to ask you to do may seem a little strange, but we're trying to become acquainted with how the body works and the changes we can make in our muscles.

2. I'd like you to simply open and close one of your hands several times. Look at the muscles in the forearm as you do so. You can actually see them working. Keep opening and closing the hand and take your other hand and place it around your forearm, just below the elbow. Now you can *feel* the muscles working.

3. Squeeze your hand as hard as you can. With your other hand you can feel how tight the forearm has become. Then let the hand relax completely, as limply as you can. Do you feel the difference now?

4. Clench your hand as tightly as you can again, and feel the muscles. Now let the hand relax slowly — very slowly. Ease the tension out of the hand, and feel how the hardness slowly leaves the forearm. Feel how the muscles are slowly giving way. Then bring the tension back again, slowly. Begin to clench your fist again. Gradually make it very tight. Feel how the hardness and stiffness have returned to the forearm.

5. See, now, if you can make your arm about half as tight as it was. Try to be halfway between total relaxation and total tension. What does it feel like? Let your mind be aware of the feeling you have now. Then tighten your hand again; then let it go completely limp. Notice the differences in the tension. Change the amount of tension in your arm in any way you like now, going from tight to relaxed to tight to tighter. As you do so, try to *feel* all the different amounts of tension. Keep changing the tension, but stop sometimes and hold the amount of stiffness in your arm for a few seconds. Keep it steady, and let your mind sense how tight it is. Then, when you stop again, notice the difference in feeling from the last tension you had.

(These explorations are focused on the kinesthetic phenomenon of "just noticeable differences" which was described earlier. The attention of students is directed to the feedback information they are receiving from their own muscles. The schema presented can be expanded in scope and can be used with other muscle groups in the body, or with the entire body. Always, however, the critical concern is to *focus students' attention on the internal feedback available to them* and also to *facilitate a sensory recognition of the changes in the feedback.*)

6. We have seen how we can change the amount of tension we have in our muscles. The muscles can be very stiff or very relaxed or anything in between. And of course, we can make those same changes when we are moving. To feel these changes in tension, imagine that you are picking up a very heavy weight. It is so heavy you can hardly lift it. But you can get it off the floor, and you can finally lift it over your head. Feel how much tension it takes to lift this weight. Now imagine that you are lifting a very light weight from the floor, one that weighs hardly annything at all. You find that you can easily get this weight over your head. In fact, you can throw it into the air and catch it again. Do that — throw it up and catch it. Then throw it all the way to the other side of the room. But now let's say that you have the heavy weight in your hands again. Try to throw this one into the air and catch it again. Can you throw the heavy one across the room?

7. The body seems to do what it needs to do. When we lift a light weight the body does different things from those it does when we lift a heavy weight. Not only that, but we can actually *tell* the body what to do. In fact, you just did so. There was no weight in your hands, but you *told* your body what to do.

8. Now, let's see how we can tell the body what to do as we move around in the room. First, let's make the body very strong and move around the room very forcefully. Move with hard, powerful motion. Stop sometimes to feel how very tight all your muscles are at that moment. Change your position as you move — sometimes very high and sometimes very low. Stomp your feet with each step. Then, try to move very quietly while still being very strong.

9. Now, let some of the tension out of the body. Feel yourself starting to be more relaxed as you move. It seems as if you are losing some of your body weight and becoming lighter. More and more it is getting easier for you to move. You are almost beginning to float. Feel how relaxed your muscles are becoming. There isn't much tension anymore. You are *telling* your muscles to relax, and you are using only enough energy to keep you moving. It's all easy now.

10. Next, try changing the tension in your body as you move, doing so in any way that you wish. Make yourself very strong or very light, whatever you please. Keep feeling the differences in your muscles as you make these changes. Notice how you can tell the tension to come out of the muscles in your legs — or you can put it back into your legs. Feel the changes as you make them in your back — in your arms — in your fingers — and even in your face.

11. And now, as you are moving, I am going to suggest certain things for you to do. You will need to listen carefully, because some of them may be difficult, and sometimes there will be two things to do at once. First, try using any part of your body, or even your whole body, to make a movement that is very strong and very fast. Next, do a movement that is weak and slow. Then try one that is slow but strong; then fast and weak. Then do a strong motion that is very high, and a slow motion that is very low. And now here's a difficult one: Try to do a motion that changes as you do it. Start off slowly and become very fast. Then start slowly, become fast, and then slow down again. Try a motion that is weak at the beginning and becomes very strong. Do one that is slow and strong at the beginning and then becomes fast and weak. Then try one that is slow and weak at first and becomes fast and strong.

12. When we play many sports, the movements we make are not only of one kind. Often we need to execute actions which need changes in intensity throughout. For example, when we hit a softball or a baseball, the swing we use does not travel at the same speed from beginning to end. Instead, it increases in force. I'd like us all to try to feel that now. Imagine you have a baseball bat in your hands. Swing your imaginary bat back and forth for awhile, trying actually to feel its weight. Then, swing as if you were trying to hit a ball. Do some more swings, trying each time to sense your muscles increasing the speed of the bat as you bring it into the ball. Feel the impact of the ball and the thrust of the bat as you hit through the ball. There's that phrase — *through the ball*. You'll hear it many times in your life — when you are learning softball or tennis or golf or any other sport where you are striking an object. Now you're actually feeling it. You are doing so by increasing the speed of your movement as you swing the imaginary bat.

(Again, the principle of just noticeable differences applies here. Students should be asked to make movements intentionally

61

different from the accelerated force of the baseball swing for the specific purpose of being able to kinesthetically recognize the differences.)

13. Now, let's think about another sport. How about sprinting — running as fast as you can for a short distance. In such an event we must also *accelerate* a movement. Only this time the whole body is involved, not just the arms. I'd like you to see if you can use the same feeling of increasing the speed of a movement as you did when you were swinging the imaginary baseball bat — put that feeling into your whole body. Every part of you can now help to produce the acceleration. Take a stance that you think can give you the best start. Try to run as fast as you can for a short distance out of that stance. Try different stances. Try with your feet apart, then close together, one foot in front of the other, and then the other foot forward. As you come out of the stance, notice how you can use your arms to give the body extra power. Can you do anything with your knees? Where should you have your head? Can you feel how *explosive* your whole self is in this exploration?

14. In sports we do not always run at such a sudden acceleration. Sometimes we must do *controlled* running, as when we play in a basketball game. There are times in the game when we need to move at only a medium speed; then, in an instant, we may need to run very hard but soon are back to a slower pace again. Sometimes we must move sideways or backward or use our force to jump as high as we can. We are going to do all these things now, seeing how well we can tell the body what to do. First, imagine that you are playing a basketball game and you are moving slowly up the court, when suddenly. . . .

BACK TO THE BACKSWING

A few pages ago we left a bewildered tennis player trying to correct a too-big backswing. Now, a few lessons later, we'll eavesdrop again.

TEACHER: Now that you have changed your exaggerated backswing, I've got a new thing I'd like you to try. It's something that needs the same attention to your internal information system that you used to discipline your backswing. It's also a *feeling*. It will help you to get more power into your stroke.

SANDY: Great! I sure could use some of that.

TEACHER: Power in tennis, or in any other sport, is all a matter of timing. At least, that's what everybody says. But what they really mean is that at the time you hit the ball, your racket must be gaining in speed. It must be *accelerating*.

SANDY: I guess mine isn't doing that.

TEACHER: I don't think so. What does the ball usually feel like when you hit it?

SANDY: Ah, well, like a ball? I'm not sure what you mean.

TEACHER: Does it feel heavy on your racket?

SANDY: Heavy? Well, yes, it does. But that's because I have weak wrists, and the racket keeps twisting in my hand.

TEACHER: I can understand that you feel that way. But very few persons have weak wrists. They may *seem* weak, but that's because your racket is not accelerating when you hit the ball. The fact that your racket turns in your hand when you hit the ball is caused by the weight of the ball overpowering the weight of your racket. It's all physics. When two objects in motion strike each other, one usually overpowers the other. If your racket is gaining momentum at the moment of impact, however, it will overcome the weight and speed of the ball. Even if you hit the ball off center, the racket will have so much force behind it that it will not turn in your hand. Let's give it a try. Hit a few ground strokes, and as you do, notice the feel of your racket head as you hit the ball. Give your attention to what your body is telling you about the moment of contact.

(*A dozen ground strokes later . . .*)

SANDY: I'm trying it, but I'm not really certain that I am feeling what I'm supposed to feel.

TEACHER: Does the ball feel as if it has the weight of a rock when you hit it?

SANDY: Well, yes. Certainly more like a rock than a feather.

TEACHER: OK. Now I'd like you to swing the racket without hitting a ball. Try to sense a feeling of rhythm as you swing. The rhythm is one that increases in speed as you bring the racket forward. Try not to force it, but just let it *happen*. Give your body the freedom to swing, without trying to mechanically *think* your way through it.

That's great. Can you feel the acceleration?

SANDY: Yes, I actually think I can.

TEACHER: You see, you are now placing your attention on the moving parts of your body. Try a few swings in slow motion, still giving some acceleration to the foreswing. You might be particularly aware of certain muscles while you do so. You are getting to know every inch of your swing, and you are feeling what it is like to accelerate forward. Now magnify that feeling. Swing your racket forward with more and more velocity, increasing the acceleration each time. There! You can even hear it swishing through the air.

SANDY: Wow! I'd hit every ball over the fence swinging like this.

TEACHER: You might. When you give your attention to the sensations of your arm and your body, you are able to develop "touch" in your game. That's the ability to control the amount of force you put on your racket and the capacity to direct the ball more accurately. I'm going to hit some balls to you now, and as you return them, keep your attention on the feel of your arm as you swing forward to meet the ball. Use the same sensation of acceleration you just showed. Never mind what happens to the ball. Just try to experience the *feel* of the motion.

             (*Bounce–thump. Bounce–whack. Bounce–crack. Bounce–smash.*)

SANDY: This is great! Look at the ball! I've never hit it so powerfully before.

TEACHER: It's all because you are both *listening* to your body and *allowing* it to do what you would like it to do.

SANDY: I think you have just worked a miracle on me.

TEACHER: No, not I. *You* deserve the credit. That's the beauty of this kind of learning. You are learning by listening to yourself and not to someone else telling you how you must swing.

(More of this technique may be found in *The Inner Game of Tennis* by W. Timothy Gallwey [New York: Random House, 1974].)

In the learning of all sports skills, it is critical to become sensitive to all body parts and their actions in execution. To do so, one must become extraordinarily aware of the feel of the activity. In tennis, this awareness even projects onto the racket head. Indirectly, through the feedback system of kinesthesis, it becomes possible to *know* where the racket head is and what it is doing by actually *feeling* it. This is a general ability that we all had as children; as adults it may be difficult to recapture. But we can help others — our students — to keep and use this sensation before it is lost. We can do so as simply as may be necessary. We might not have any equipment, but all we need is an unobstructed space. We may not be experienced in technique, but all we need is verbal inventiveness. Thus, in an open space, with nothing but suggestions, we can have students experiment with and experience their individual movement potentials.

A LONG TIME AGO IN A FARAWAY PLACE

In the traditionally accepted view of the learning of motor performance, students are expected to program specific movement patterns into their nervous systems, store them in a biological stockpile somewhere, and retrieve them at some appropriate time in the future. This may be a relatively reasonable expectation when considering the performance of a skill which can be executed in a dependable environment. For example, a competitive gymnast can rely on stable conditions (never any wind, or temperature changes, or downhill lies, or other players or objects in motion). The gymnast can therefore perform well-rehearsed and formal movements without the need to react to constantly changing environmental conditions. Most other motor performances, however, occur in unstable circumstances. The environment in most sports is always changing, and there is a correlated need for performers to react to such change. The traditional view of performance, if correct, would require the learning and memory storage of an infinite number of movement patterns, each one ready to be selectively put into use. This, in fact, is the contention of a widely accepted earlier concept of motor performance (Henry 1960). Even an accomplished gymnast, however, must at some point rely on kinesthetic feedback to make the minor changes in routines which are a part of refinement. Physical performance never quite reaches the point of being a mere discharge of a pattern completely mastered at an earlier time. Always, human beings remain human beings, not machines.

Accordingly, while the traditional teaching of specific movement patterns does have its place, it most certainly does not have the *entire* place. Versatility and adaptability are more lasting and usable for the lifetime performance of motor skills. The competitive gymnastic season eventually ends, as do external demands for precise motor execution, and ultimately everyone falls back into the pleasures of movement for its own sake. Perfection loses importance as pure enjoyment slowly takes its place. Thus we see the typical pattern of a lifelong relation with our own body. We first use it spontaneously. As children we were most completely ourselves;

mind and body were one. Then, at some later time in our lives, we lose this closeness with the physical being. Still later, when the mind is not so cluttered with the static demands of routine life, we make attempts to recapture the honesty of the free physical self we knew earlier. Is it not conceivable that if we had maintained a kinesthetic interest in the physical person throughout the learning years, we would have a much better chance of calling on that talent some bright spring day when our neighbor talked us into the first golf we have played in four years?

TALKING TO THE BODY

The real advantage of movement education is the new dimension it adds to mind–body interactions. There is the development of a psychodynamic energy which can constantly gauge the voltage of muscle activity. The mind becomes capable of responding directly and specifically to the information it is being fed by the dancing of hundreds of thousands of muscle cell impulses.

That's only part of the story, however. In the final act, the mind can *alter* the states of muscle events to satisfy the moment-by-moment demands. The mind not only receives information, it also sends information.

Exactly how does one get to the final step of *telling* the muscles how to work? Movement education intends to teach people not only how to *receive* information but also how to *use* that information to affect motor responses. How can this best be done?

For one thing, we must communicate with the body in language it understands. The body does not really know English or French or Esperanto. Its native language is *feeling*. It communicates by *sensation*. Consequently, if we talk to the body in normal verbalizations, those verbalizations must get translated into sensations before they can be understood. Thus, we cannot necessarily *tell* the body what to do in the same way that we can talk to another person about math or history or the weather.

Even in those moments when we liberate our minds for the pure brainstorming of daydreaming, we tend to channel our thoughts into language. Yet when we want to execute a motor performance, words can get in the way. If we want a strike in the tenth frame, we cannot talk the body into it by saying, "OK, body, do your pushaway first. Then take the ball back on the second step, keep your shoulders straight, your eyes on the target, bring the ball on a direct line for that target, and follow through." Instead, we must simply ask the body to send the ball into the pocket.

What?

We start by not using words, or at least by using as few as possible. Rather, we must use *images*. We must imagine our performance. We must *see* it and *feel* it as we see it. And that's a nonverbal affair. There is no language that can describe it. We do it without any need for words.

And so here we are with a group of thirty students in front of us, whom we are trying to help use their bodies better. We've got to say *something* to them. We can't just stand there without using any words at all. As soon as we say something, however, we run the risk that the words we use to describe any movement will get bounced around in thirty brains and come out with thirty different interpretations. We can't say to all students, "Keep your left arm straight," if we are teaching them how to hit a golf ball, expecting that it has the same connotation for everyone. What is *straight*? Is it a locked arm? Is it a comfortably extended arm? Is it a hyperextended arm?

Furthermore, there is enough evidence (see especially Marteniuk 1976) to let us know that the more a teacher verbalizes about the "how" of motor execution, the more student perceptions tend to be drawn into mechanical ways of thinking about motor events. It may even be better, in the teaching of certain motor performances, to simply demonstrate the execution and say *nothing* about the mechanics. In this way, each student can receive the stimulus of the demonstration with his/her own reference system — an individually private way to sense the movement with personal physiological language. Such a procedure is a nonverbal means of communicating about a nonverbal event.

Yet, the matter isn't quite so simple. Any teacher who wishes to enhance student perceptions of the sensory aspects of motor performance must intentionally direct attention to those aspects. Words are required. This is the real reason why the teaching technique of movement education is verbally *suggestive* and why it *allows* individual interpretation of the words. This technique is a safeguard against the potential misrepresentation of verbal communication.

Thus, the important teaching factor in movement education is to supply the body with *meaningful* information. Since the methodology is based on exploration, problem solving, and self-appropriated learnings, the information provided by the teacher must necessarily be open-ended. This is another reminder that the art of movement education is to be a stimulator rather than a dictator.

CREATIONS AND CONCLUSIONS

One of the more widely stated attributes of movement education is its supposed benefits in fostering creativity. Students who experience the methods of self-discovery are believed to somehow become more spontaneous, expressive, and inventive. Is there evidence to support this claim?

The picture is a fairly complex one. First of all, it must be recognized that there is no universally accepted definition of creativity; hence there are no measures which have been widely used as tests for its presence. Additionally, it is important to distinguish between spontaneity and creativity. Whatever creativity may be, it is something more than spontaneity. When students in a movement education class are expressing free images and ideas, it does not necessarily mean they are being creative. If they do nothing more than execute these free expressions, then they are only *experiencing* them — which is not enough to qualify as creativity. A more legitimate display of creativity is seen when students actualize their internal selves to do original things, presenting new responses to familiar situations, with unexpected connections occurring between events without preplanning. This type of response is a desirable enlargement of human experience which places no restraints on the inner self. It is a spiritually induced and spiritually endowed art — a power of the soul rather than of pure mind.

The evidence of the educational influence on creativity is spotty. Nonetheless, there is some indication that an attention to the purposeful teaching of creativity can, in fact, result in an increase in original thinking (Eberle 1969; Schmidt, Goforth, and Drew 1975; Larsen 1976). This may be particularly true for students with learning handicaps (Torrance and Torrance 1972; Schmais 1976). When the intent of teaching is directed toward the expression of creativity through a motor medium, it appears that the efforts can indeed be successful (Rugg 1963; Massialas and Zevin 1967; Feldhusen and Hobson 1972; Lieberman 1977). However, these increases in motor creativity cannot be expected to transfer into a correlated improvement in skill execution (Stroup and Pielstick 1965; Philipp 1969).

The most comprehensive collections of research relating to educational attempts at fostering creativity have been assembled by Torrance (see especially Torrance and Myers 1972). Essentially, the overall conclusion emanating from these writings is that education has had a more adverse than positive effect on creativity. However, there *have* been successes; and Torrance indicates that the effective programs seem to have certain characteristics in common, among which are the following: (1) the teacher respects unusual student questions, (2) the teacher encourages and respects unusual answers to questions, (3) students recognize that their individual ideas have value, (4) the educational environment is arranged to promote self-initiated learning, and (5) the educational environment provides periods of nonevaluated experimentation in learning.

Some research has approached the study of creativity by attempting to analyze the thought patterns which give rise to creative ideas. One such pattern which has been identified is called *divergent thinking*. This particular capacity refers to the ability to generate a number of possible solutions to a problem and apparently has a very predictable relationship to creative abilities (Feldhusen, Treffinger, and Elias 1970). Interestingly, this mode of thinking is specifically stimulated in the methodology of movement education where the teacher frequently challenges students: "Find a different way to do it," or "Discover three different ways to do the same thing," or "Is there a better way to do it?"

Divergent thinking ability seems to be a quality that can be specifically fostered (Taylor 1972; Luthe 1976; Scandura 1977). An interesting feature in the successful learning of this ability is the individual's willingness to lower the threshold of ideas which are considered worthy (Maier 1970). In this respect, divergent thinkers become cognitively less inhibited, being more openly receptive to a variety of possible ways to consider the same problem (Martindale 1975). Intriguingly, one technique which apparently generates a willingness to lower these resistance thresholds is simply that of having more than one person work on a problem at the same time (Richards 1974; Stein 1974). Two or more persons working together seem to have the effect both of lowering the thresholds and of increasing the variety of considerations for solutions to problems.

CASTLES IN THE AIR

In the final analysis, movement education may be a means for the development of creativity, and then again it may not be. The real research evidence is not yet available. Between the hypothetical writings which are so plentiful and the legitimate research which is so scarce, there is little to give substance to the widely accepted notion that creative abilities are a natural or purposeful outcome of movement education programs.

In a most comprehensive and analytical work on creativity, Arieti (1976) repeatedly reminds us of the complexity of the whole affair and the accompanying difficulty of establishing valid research procedures for the study of creativity. The problem may begin (and end) with the very confusion that exists relative to what actually constitutes creativity. Just because it cannot be universally defined does not mean creativity doesn't exist. Not everything which exists in life needs proof of its existence. Even in the disciplined world of pure research, there is room for intuition. The reasonable midpoint of opinion may be that the matter of creativity and its potential development are educational endeavors which may or may not be intended objectives.

AN ASSEMBLAGE OF COOPERATION

If the divergent thinking which leads to creative behavior can best be catalyzed through group effort, then movement education should provide opportunities for partner or group experiences. The same exploratory and problem-solving attitude can be established, the only change being that problems are now directed toward cooperative solutions. For example, two partners might be presented with suggestions such as the following:

1. One partner forms a bridge with his/her body. The other partner goes over and under this bridge. Use a variety of ways to make the bridges and a variety of ways to go over and under them.

2. One partner forms a bridge; the other goes over or under and then forms a new bridge, with the first partner going over or under in a way that is different from the method first used. A sequence could be used, each partner forming a different bridge each time, with the passage over and under also changed.

3. One partner forms any shape and then moves toward the other partner who must go over, under, or around, according to the possibilities presented. (The first partner should not always remain on the feet when moving, but use leaps, rolling, etc.)

4. One partner establishes a repeated sequential movement (such as some kind of waving of the arms, or a rocking motion); the other partner moves around, or from one side to the other, timing the movement to avoid or move through the sequence set up by the first partner.

5. One partner helps the other to achieve a balance which could not otherwise be attained.

6. One partner acts as a solid piece of apparatus, maintaining a steady, unyielding base. The other balances on the first partner, getting the weight completely off the floor.

7. One partner maintains a steady, unyielding base. The other achieves momentary flight by using the first partner as an assist (leapfrog is a beginning example). A sequence could be used.

8. As one partner maintains a balance, the other partner tries to interrupt the balance. The first partner senses the pressure from the other and makes adjustments. (This is not intended to be a violent activity.) A variety of balance positions and body parts for support should be used.

9. Both partners form a balance, the stability of which is interdependent on each other. The partners then raise or lower themselves or rotate or move about, trying constantly to maintain their common balance.

10. Both partners form a common balance by using forces that pull away from each other. (The most simplified example would be clasping hands and leaning away from each other.) The two then invent a variety of shapes and use a variety of contact points always maintaining balance with the use of opposing forces.

With the addition of a few lengths of rope, one for each two students, problems such as the following could be posed:

1. What shapes can the two of you make while holding on to the rope? Can you move from one shape into another? Can you make moving shapes together?

2. If each partner holds an end of the rope, how large a space can the two of you use?

3. Can you influence the movement of your partner by the way that you use the rope? Can you resist your partner's influence on you?

4. How many different ways can you and your partner jump over the rope without letting go? Now travel around the room, jumping over the rope as you go.

5. See if you can get from one side of the rope to the other by having it pass over your heads. Now, just one of you hold the rope and do the same. Can one of you hold or swing the rope so that the other can jump over it?

If hoops are available (one for each two students), they offer some different possibilities.

1. You and your partner roll the hoop to each other. Now throw and catch. Can you get the hoop to your partner in a different way each time, sometimes on the floor and sometimes in the air?

71

2. One of you hold the hoop while the other jumps through. Hold it sometimes horizontally, sometimes vertically. Can you jump through the hoop with different body parts leading each time?

3. One of you take a beanbag and try to throw it through the hoop while the other person rolls it. Can you work as a team?

4. One of you roll the hoop while the other person tries to go through the hoop as it is rolling. Can you roll the hoop in such a way as to help your partner through it? Can you make the hoop spin so that it will come back to you? Can the other person go through the hoop at just the moment when it begins to change directions?

5. What shapes can the two of you make while both are holding on to the hoop? when one is inside the hoop and the other outside? when both are inside?

A CARBON COPY

One way of relating to another person without being dependent on the person to assist in movement executions is by following or copying. In this scheme one person performs a movement, and the other responds by following or copying. Properly handled, this technique is more than an imitation of another's movement; it is rather an additional way of focusing attention on body parts and recognizing the sequences within movements. Moreover, each partner can be a challenge to the other, offering movements which are within the capacity of the other person while still demanding skillful execution. Students can work as partners, or in small groups where the leader uses all the variances of balance, body shape, speed, force, and other movement dimensions for others to replicate.

Partner performances could also be matched, where two or more students attempt to do the same movement simultaneously. In these endeavors one student exactly duplicates another's direction, intensity, length of stride, so that the movement is performed as a coordinated and mirrored execution.

There is an interesting (although speculative) potential in these techniques. As each person tries to follow or duplicate the movements of another, the responses required will probably be different from the person's normal ways of moving. Every human being has an inherently determined performance pattern — a certain pace with which each of us seems to feel comfortable. We have preferred ways of walking, driving, playing a tennis match. External demands, however, will frequently force an alteration in individual style, with a need to motorically adapt to environmental conditions. This situation is no different from that of a basketball team which plays a slow-down game against a team that likes to play racehorse-style and thereby forces the latter team to change its pace. Adaptability thus becomes an asset. In this context, some research (see especially Hallahan and Cruickshank 1973) has indicated that certain learning disabilities are associated with an inability to make the motoric adjustments required by changing environmental conditions. Could movement education help in making these adjustments? There is, quite frankly, no good evidence to show that it does help. Neither is there research to show that it does not help, however, and reason leads one to believe that it should.

Another hidden possibility may be seen in the factor of laterality, a perceptual quality which is the ability to distinguish the left side of the body from the right side and to control these sides independently or simultaneously. This aspect of motor development has been attended to most emphatically by Kephart (1960). In his view the learning of laterality will transfer into enhanced reading abilities, preventing, in particular, the often seen visual laterality problem of reversing certain letters, most notably b and d. Once again, there is not enough research to support an unqualified acceptance of the idea that motor programs can assist reading ability, but there is an indication that they might. (Hallahan and Cruickshank 1973). So it may be that when one student stands in front of another performing certain laterality movements which are duplicated by the other student, a subtle perceptive awareness is growing which may not be immediately apparent. (A series of suggested activities for laterality development may be found in Chaney and Kephart 1968.)

NEW WINE AND NEW BOTTLES

There is something intrinsically appealing about games. But there is nothing sacred about their structure. Take, for example, the use of a volleyball — a balloon could substitute, or a beach ball, or anything that slows the pace of the game. Bruner (1963) once said something to the effect that you could teach something about anything to anyone at any time. As applied to the movement education program, this means that a game can be adapted to the abilities of participants. The receipt and propulsion which are part of volleyball play can best be learned by novice performers when the flight of the ball allows learners enough time to focus on the task. With some ingenuity, virtually all games can be adapted in this or other ways.

And how about this version — leave the volleyball nets up, but give each team a blanket. A blanket? The team holds the blanket like a firefighter's net and then in unison tosses a ball of some kind over the net to be caught by the other team — with their blanket. A point is scored when the ball is successfully tossed and caught. A point, that is, for *both* sides. There is no winner. *And* there is no loser. This is part of a new approach to movement awareness called "new games," the purpose of which is to provide situations of a "no-lose" atmosphere. The example given (and more) may be found in Orlick (1977).

To go one step further, why not let students invent their own games? Totally. They could be stimulated by giving the simple cue "I'm thinking of a game — what do you need to know to play it?" To which students may respond by inquiring, "Do we use a ball?" or, "Is there any out-of-bounds?" or, "How do we score?" The answers, of course, are anything students decide they should be.

The point is that when the appropriate time comes to learn the skills and cooperations which are a part of game play, the fundamental *attitude* of movement education need not get lost in the attention usually given to perfection and winning.

SENSING, KNOWING, AND ACTING

In movement education there are processes within processes and cycles within cycles. Nothing is old, and nothing is static. The program can exist with only an inventive teacher, some curious students, and an empty space; or it can be adapted to a high school gymnasium filled with a budget-depleting assemblage of apparatus. The method can be used for children having a first experience in externally stimulated purposeful explorations, and it can be helpful to the skilled golfer trying to perfect a draw.

Always, the technique is the same — to provide an environment in which learners become sensitive to their own internal feedback, with the resulting ability of interpreting that feedback and the final product of improved control over motor responses. It is a conscious venture using internal information to determine how effectively the processing system is functioning; and it is a physical answer to the classic Greek declaration that the highest function in life is to "know thyself."

Much is a neurological phenomenon; how all can be accomplished remains a mystery. The explanations of feedback are well documented, but they tell us only what *has* happened. They are post facto, for the neural information supplied to the brain comes as a *result* of movement; neurophysiology tells us nothing about the mental activities which can *influence* the intentional control of muscle activity. It's like studying an emotion. There are not so many chemical changes in the blood or so many hills and valleys to show up on an oscilloscope to give evidence of its real workings. However, the scientific world accepts the notion that the emotion is *there*. Most importantly, it's there for everyone. And in these days of mainstreaming, when an educational scheme presents the same potential, the same opportunity, and the same objectives for all involved, that factor alone makes it worthy of attention.

The interest generated by movement education is deserved. Movement education is an effective technique for the learning of true sensations and the voluntary control of energy. Its potential is probably greater than now realized. It may, in fact, be a step toward a new reality.

We are all familiar with the repressive constraints exerted on our physical selves. We need only turn on the television to be reminded how we can disguise, camouflage, distort, and otherwise deny the physical person. Additionally, our medicine cabinets contain many items to make us forget our inner sensations.

Probably each of us is physically only half the person we ought to be. We are making use of only a portion of our physical resources. But just as we need not be sick to get better, movement education does not attempt to show us where we are wrong; rather, it shows us how we can make things more right.

A CARRY-OVER CONSIDERATION

Often, motor activities are considered to have rather generalized "carry-over" value. This means that the nature of a particular activity is such that it is likely to become a lifetime interest for many people. Activities traditionally thought of in this context include golf, tennis, bowling, and the like.

In a real sense, movement education has great carry-over. In fact, it carries over into carry-over activities as well as into *all* activities. To be more precise, it carries over *into* everything. A learning which is as basic, as general yet specific, and as widely usable as self-knowing is a supreme carry-over, for it can be applied *in* all motor events. Thus, that chip shot on the eighteenth green, or the ace in the tiebreaker game, or the spare in the tenth frame may not be so far removed from us. Even more importantly, we may have found (and we can help others to find) an intimate contact with the inner self. If nothing else, we have brought the brain and the body more closely together.

REFERENCES

Anthony, Jeanne. "Classroom Performance Improved Through Movement." *Academic Therapy Quarterly* 6, no. 4 (Summer 1971): 423–31.

Arieti, Silvano. *Creativity, the Magic Synthesis.* New York: Basic Books, 1976.

Arnett, Chappelle. *All Active, All Successful: Developing Teacher Compentency in Elementary School Physical Education.* Bellingham, Wash.: Educational Designs and Consultants, 1976.

Baker, Barbara A. *Movement Education for Students with Special Needs in Physical Education.* Arlington County Public Schools, Va. December 1973.

Barsch, Ray H. *Achieving Perceptual-Motor Efficiency: A Space-Oriented Approach to Learning.* Seattle: Special Child Publications, 1968.

Block, Susan Dimond. *"Me and I'm Great": Physical Education for Children Three Through Eight.* Minneapolis: Burgess Publishing Co., 1977.

Briggs, Megan M. *Movement Education: The Place of Movement in Physical Education.* Boston: Plays, 1975.

Brown, Barbara. *Stress and the Art of Biofeedback.* New York: Harper and Row, 1977.

Bruner, Jerome S. *The Process of Education.* Cambridge, Mass.: Harvard University Press, 1963.

Chaney, Clara M., and Kephart, Newell C. *Motoric Aids to Perceptual Training.* Columbus, Ohio: Charles E. Merrill Publishing Co., 1968.

Cole, Henry P. *Process Education: The New Direction for Elementary-Secondary Schools.* Englewood Cliffs, N.J.: Educational Technology Publications, 1972.

Davis, Martha. "Movement and Cognition." *Theory Into Practice* 16, no. 3 (June 1977): 207–10.

Dochtery, David, and Peake, Les "Creatrad: An Approach to Teaching Games." *Journal of Physical Education and Recreation* 47, no. 4 (April 1976): 20–22.

Dunkin, M. J., and Biddle, B. J. *The Study of Teaching.* New York: Holt, Rinehart and Winston, 1974.

Eberle, Robert. "Experimentation in the Teaching of Creative Thinking Processes." *Journal of Creative Behavior* 3 (Summer 1969): 219.

Eckstein, Gustav. *The Body Has a Head.* New York: Harper and Row, 1970.

Fast, Julius. *Body Language.* New York: M. Evans and Co., 1970.

Feldhusen, J. F.; Treffinger, D. J.; and Elias, R. M. "Prediction of Academic Achievement with Divergent and Convergent Thinking and Personality Variables." *Psychology in the Schools* 7 (1970): 46–52.

_____, and Hobson, Sandrak. "Freedom and Play: Catalysts for Creativity." *Elementary School Journal* 73, no. 3 (December 1972): 48.

Gagné, Robert M. *The Conditions of Learning.* New York: Holt, Rinehart and Winston, 1970.

Getman, G. N. "The Physical Educator's Role in Academic Readiness." *Foundations and Practices in Perceptual Motor Learning — A Quest for Understanding.* Washington, D.C.: American Alliance for Health, Physical Education and Recreation, 1971, pp. 61–65.

Gilbert, Anne Green. *Teaching the Three Rs Through Movement Experiences: A Handbook for Teachers.* Minneapolis: Burgess Publishing Co., 1977.

Gilliom, Bonnie Cherp. *Basic Movement Education for Children: Rationale and Teaching Units.* Reading, Mass.: Addison-Wesley Publishing Co., 1970.

Hall, E. T. *Hidden Dimension.* Garden City, N.Y.: Doubleday, 1966.

Hallahan, Daniel P., and Cruickshank, William M. *Psychoeducational Foundations of Learning Disabilities.* Englewood Cliffs, N.J.: Prentice-Hall, 1973.

Hart, Joseph T. *New Directions in Client-Centered Therapy.* Boston: Houghton Mifflin, 1970.

Havelock, R. G. *Planning for Innovation Through Dissemination and Utilization of Knowledge.* Ann Arbor, Mich.: Institute for Social Research, University of Michigan, 1969.

Henry, Franklin M. "Increased Response Latency for Complicated Movements and a Memory Drum Theory of Neuromotor Reaction." *Research Quarterly* 31 (1960): 448–58.

Jacobson, Edmund. *You Must Relax.* New York: McGraw-Hill, 1957.

Kephart, Newell C. *The Slow Learner in the Classroom.* Columbus, Ohio: Charles E. Merrill Publishing Co., 1960.

Laban, Rudolph. *Modern Educational Dance.* London: MacDonald and Evans, 1948.

————. *The Mastery of Movement.* 2nd ed. Revised by Lisa Ullman. London: MacDonald and Evans, 1960.

————, and Lawrence, F. C. *Effort.* London: MacDonald and Evans, 1947.

Larsen, Gary. "The Effects of Different Teaching Styles on Creativity." *Journal of Creative Behavior* (3d Quarter 1976): 200.

Leukel, Francis P. *Essentials of Physiological Psychology.* St. Louis: C. V. Mosby Co., 1978.

Lieberman, Nina J. *Playfulness: Its Relationship to Imagination and Creativity.* New York: Academic Press, 1977.

Luthe, Wolfgang. *Creativity Mobilization Technique.* New York: Grune and Stratton, 1976.

Maier, Norman R. F. *Problem Solving and Creativity.* Belmont, Calif.: Brooks/Cole, 1970.

Maltzman, I. "On the Training of Originality." *Psychological Review* 67 (1960): 229–42.

Marteniuk, Ronald G. *Information Processing in Motor Skills.* New York: Holt, Rinehart and Winston, 1976.

Martindale, Colin. "What Makes Creative People Different." *Psychology Today* 9, no. 2 (July 1975): 44–50.

Massialas, Byron G., and Zevin, Jack. *Creative Encounters in the Classroom.* New York: John Wiley and Sons, 1967.

McDermott, Elisabeth R. "Music and Rhythms — From Movement to Lipreading and Speech." *Volta Review* 73, no. 4 (April 1973): 229–32.

Mosston, Muska. *Teaching Physical Education.* Columbus, Ohio: Charles E. Merrill Publishing Co., 1966.

Newell, Allen, and Simon, Herbert. *Human Problem Solving.* Englewood Cliffs, N.J.: Prentice-Hall, 1972.

North, Marion. *Personality Assessment Through Movement.* Boston: Plays, 1975.

Orluck, Terry. *Competitive Insanity: Cooperative Alternatives.* Washington, D.C.: Hawkins and Associates, 1977.

Philipp, John A. "Comparison of Motor Creativity with Figural and Verbal Creativity and Selected Motor Skills." *Research Quarterly* 40 (March 1969): 163–73.

Rhodes, William C., and Tracy, Michael L. *A Study of Child Variance, Vol. 2: Interventions.* Ann Arbor, Mich.: University of Michigan, 1972.

Rickards, Tudor. *Problem Solving Through Creative Analysis.* New York: Halsted Press, 1974.

Robins, Ferris, and Robins, Jennet. "Educational Rhythmics: An Interdisciplinary Approach to Mental and Physical Disabilities." *Journal of Learning Disabilities* 5, no. 2 (February 1972): 104–9.

Rugg, Harold. "*Imagination: An Inquiry into the Sources and Conditions that Stimulate Creativity.*" Edited by Kenneth D. Benne. New York: Harper and Row, 1963.

Scandura, Joseph M. *Problem Solving: A Structural/Process Approach with Instructional Implications.* New York: Academic Press, 1977.

Schmais, Claire. "What Is Dance Therapy?" *Journal of Health, Physical Education and Recreation* 47, no. 1 (January 1976): 39.

Schmidt, Toni; Goforth, Elissa; and Drew, Kathy. "Creative Dramatics and Creativity: An Experimental Study." *Educational Theatre Journal* 27, no. 1 (March 1975): 111–14.

Schmuck, Richard; Chesler, Mark; and Lippitt, Ronald. *Problem Solving to Improve Classroom Learning.* Chicago: Science Research Associates, 1966.

Singer, Robert N. *Motor Learning and Human Performance.* New York: Macmillan, 1975.

Smith, Karl U., and Smith, Margaret Foltz. *Cybernetic Principles of Learning and Educational Design.* New York: Holt, Rinehart and Winston, 1966.

Snodgrass, Jeanne. "Self-Concept." *Journal of Health, Physical Education and Recreation* 48, no. 9 (November-December 1977): 22–23.

Stein, Morris I. *Stimulating Creativity. Vol. 1, Individual Procedures.* New York: Academic Press, 1974.

Stroup, Francis, and Pielstick, N. L. "Motor Ability and Creativity." *Perceptual and Motor Skills* 20 (February 1965): 76–78.

Taylor, Calvin W., ed. *Climate for Creativity.* New York: Pergamon Press, 1972.

Taylor, Carla. *Rhythm: A Guide for Creative Movement.* Palo Alto, Calif.: Peek Publications, 1974.

Torrance, E. P., and Myers, R. E. *Creative Learning and Teaching*. New York: Dodd, Mead, 1972.

———, and Torrance, Pansy. "Combining Creative Problem-Solving with Creative Expressive Activities in the Education of Disadvantaged Young People." *Journal of Creative Behavior* 6, no. 1 (First Quarter 1972): 1–10.

Travers, Robert M. W., ed. *Second Handbook of Research on Teaching*. Chicago: Rand McNally and Co., 1973.

RECOMMENDED READING

Caldwell, Learohn. *A Creative Approach to a Successful Elementary Physical Education Program: A Planning Guide*. Baton Rouge, La.: Legacy Publishing Co., 1977.

Capon, Jack. J. *Basic Movement Activities. Perceptual Motor Development*. Belmont, Calif.: Fearon Publishers, 1975.

Edington, D. W., and Cunningham, Lee. *Biological Awareness: Statements for Self-Discovery*. Englewood Cliffs, N.J.: Prentice-Hall, 1975.

Fandek, Ruth W. *Classroom Capers: Movement Education in the Classroom*. Designed for Children Series. Bellingham, Wash.: Educational Designs and Consultants, 1971.

Logsdon, Bette J., ed. *Physical Education for Children: A Focus on the Teaching Process*. Philadelphia: Lea and Febiger, 1977.

Mauldon, Elizabeth, and Layson, June. *Teaching Gymnastics and Body Control*, Boston: Plays, 1975.

Morris, Don. *How to Change the Games Children Play*. Minneapolis: Burgess Publishing Co., 1976.

Rasmus, Carolyn, and Fowler, John. *Movement Activities for Places and Spaces*. Washington, D.C.: American Alliance for Health, Physical Education and Recreation, 1977.

Rizzitiello, Theresa G. *An Annotated Bibliography on Movement Education*. Washington, D.C.: National Association for Sport and Physical Education, 1977.

Schurr, Evelyn L. *Movement Experiences for Children: A Humanistic Approach to Elementary School Physical Education*. Englewood Cliffs, N.J.: Prentice-Hall, 1975.

Seidel, Beverly, et al. *Sport Skills: A Conceptual Approach to Meaningful Movement*. Dubuque, Iowa: William C. Brown, 1975.

Stein, Morris I. *Stimulating Creativity. Vol. 2, Group Procedures*. New York: Academic Press, 1975.

Sweeney, Robert T., ed. *Selected Readings in Movement Education*. Reading, Mass.: Addison-Wesley Publishing Co., 1970.

Tillotson, Joan, et al. *A Program of Movement Education for the Plattsburg Elementary Public School*. Washington, D.C.: U.S. Office of Education, HEW (OEG 66-1924, SED 320), 1969.

Werner, Peter H., and Simmons, Richard A. *Inexpensive Physical Education Equipment*. Minneapolis: Burgess Publishing Co., 1976.